DIGITAL LITERACY
Made Simple

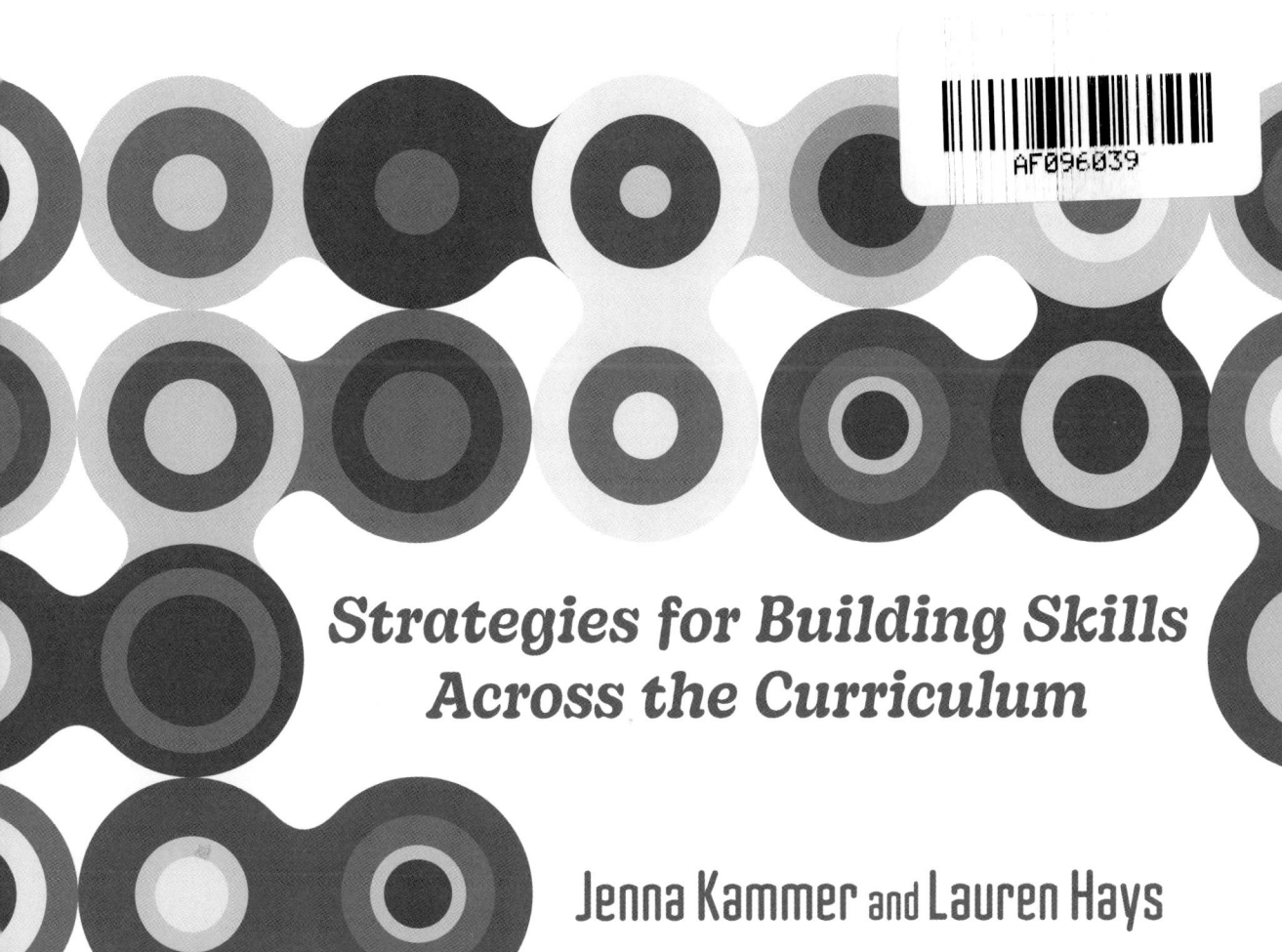

Strategies for Building Skills Across the Curriculum

Jenna Kammer and Lauren Hays

International Society for Technology in Education

PORTLAND, OREGON • ARLINGTON, VIRGINIA

DIGITAL LITERACY MADE SIMPLE
Strategies for Building Skills Across the Curriculum

Jenna Kammer and Lauren Hays

© 2023 International Society for Technology in Education

World rights reserved. No part of this book may be reproduced or transmitted in any form or by any means—electronic, mechanical, photocopying, recording, or by any information storage or retrieval system—without prior written permission from the publisher. Email permissions@iste.org for more information.

Director of Books and Journals: Emily Reed
Senior Acquisitions Editor: Valerie Witte
Development and Copy Editor: Linda Laflamme
Proofreader: Emily Padgett
Indexer: Valerie Haynes Perry
Book Design and Production: Danielle Foster
Cover Design: Christina DeYoung

Library of Congress Cataloging-in-Publication Data

Names: Kammer, Jenna, author. | Hays, Lauren, author.
Title: Digital literacy made simple : strategies for building skills across the curriculum / Jenna Kammer and Lauren Hays.
Description: First edition. | Portland, Oregon : International Society for Technology in Education, [2024] | Includes bibliographical references and index.
Identifiers: LCCN 2023036529 (print) | LCCN 2023036530 (ebook) | ISBN 9798888370087 (paperback) | ISBN 9798888370094 (epub) | ISBN 9798888370100 (pdf)
Subjects: LCSH: Computer literacy--Study and teaching--United States. | Computer-assisted instruction--United States. | Education--Data processing--Study and teaching.
Classification: LCC LB1028.43 .K36 2024 (print) | LCC LB1028.43 (ebook) | DDC 371.33/40973--dc23/eng/20230823
LC record available at https://lccn.loc.gov/2023036529
LC ebook record available at https://lccn.loc.gov/2023036530

First Edition

ISBN: 979-8-88837-008-7

Ebook version available

Printed in the United States of America

ISTE® is a registered trademark of the International Society for Technology in Education.

About ISTE

The International Society for Technology in Education (ISTE) is home to a passionate community of global educators who believe in the power of technology to transform teaching and learning, accelerate innovation and solve tough problems in education.

ISTE inspires the creation of solutions and connections that improve opportunities for all learners by delivering: practical guidance, evidence-based professional learning, virtual networks, thought-provoking events and the ISTE Standards. ISTE is also the leading publisher of books focused on technology in education. For more information or to become an ISTE member, visit iste.org. Subscribe to ISTE's YouTube channel and connect with ISTE on Twitter/X, Facebook and LinkedIn.

Related ISTE Titles

Ethics in a Digital World: Guiding Students Through Society's Biggest Questions
By Kristen Mattson

Developing Digital Detectives: Essential Lessons for Discerning Fact from Fiction in the 'Fake News' Era
By Jennifer LaGarde and Darren Hudgins

To see all books available from ISTE, please visit iste.org/books.

About the Authors

Jenna Kammer, PhD, is an associate professor and program coordinator at the University of Central Missouri in the Library Science program where she teaches classes on information resources, organizing information, and technology in libraries. Her research interests include information and digital policy and its impact on teaching and learning. Prior to becoming a professor, Jenna worked as an instructional designer and reference librarian. She is a co-editor of the book *Digital Literacy in the Disciplines*.

Lauren Hays, PhD, is an associate professor of instructional technology at the University of Central Missouri where she teaches classes on emerging technologies, leadership, and research. Her research interests include digital literacy, information literacy, and the scholarship of teaching and learning. Prior to her current position, Lauren worked as an academic librarian. She is a co-editor of the book *Digital Literacy in the Disciplines*.

Acknowledgments

Author Acknowledgments

We would like to thank the reviewers of the book for their feedback, as well as the many contributors to the book who shared their simple strategies.

Publisher Acknowledgments

ISTE gratefully acknowledges the contributions of the following:

ISTE Standards reviewers

Kira Brennan

Mary Mehsikomer

Manuscript reviewers

Robert Burggraaf

Laurie Guyon

Cammie Kannekens

Nicole Zumpano

Dedication

We would like to dedicate this book to our kids: William and Graham (Lauren) and Noah and Leif (Jenna).

Contents

Introduction ... ix

CHAPTER 1
Understanding Digital Literacy for Your Classroom

Digital Literacy Defined ... 2
What Research Says ... 5
The Core Elements of Digital Literacy ... 7
The Problem of Digital Literacy in Schools ... 11
Teaching Digital Literacy in Schools ... 12
A Portrait of a Digitally Literate Teacher ... 14
The End Game: A Portrait of a Digitally Literate Student ... 15
Chapter 1 Takeaways ... 17
Reflection ... 17

CHAPTER 2
Digital Literacy as a Simple Strategy

Teaching Digital Literacy Simply ... 20
Simple Ways to Include Digital Literacy ... 28
Chapter 2 Takeaways ... 30
Reflection ... 30

CHAPTER 3
Creating Integrated Digital Literacy Experiences

Where to Start? ... 32
Opportunities: Old and New ... 42
Build Community with Digital Experiences ... 49
Examples of Integrated Digital Literacy ... 50
The Research ... 53
Chapter 3 Takeaways ... 54
Reflection ... 54

CHAPTER 4
Developing a Culture of Digital Literacy

Digital Literacy Is Contextual	56
Challenges to Teaching Digital Literacy	56
Collaborating Across the School for Digital Literacy	59
Collaboration Between Educators	62
Interdependence: Support for a Digital Learning Culture	68
Incorporating the Simple Strategy of Building a Digital Culture	69
The Research	70
Chapter 4 Takeaways	71
Reflection	71

CHAPTER 5
Modeling Digital Literacy

What Is Modeling?	74
Modeling: A Simple Strategy	75
Incorporating the Simple Strategy of Modeling	86
The Research	88
Chapter 5 Takeaways	89
Reflection	90

CHAPTER 6
Mentoring for Digital Literacy

Mentoring: A Simple Strategy	92
Mentoring Through Discussion Groups	100
Examples of Mentoring Aligned to Digital Literacy Skills	101
Incorporating the Simple Strategy of Mentoring	102
Digital Literacy Mentoring Programs	103
The Research	104
Chapter 6 Takeaways	104
Reflection	105

CHAPTER 7
Simple Digital Literacy Strategies Across the Curriculum

Digital Literacy Case Studies	108
CASE STUDY 1 Analyzing News and Media Sources	109
CASE STUDY 2 Flattening the Latin Word	113
CASE STUDY 3 AI or Human (Expert)	115
CASE STUDY 4 Making the Case for Photo Credits	117
CASE STUDY 5 The Digital Tattoo Strategy	120
CASE STUDY 6 Navigating Databases with Digital Breadcrumbs	122
CASE STUDY 7 Lateral Reading	124
CASE STUDY 8 Accessing Research in a Filtered School	126
CASE STUDY 9 Five-Minute Tips to Teach Digital Literacy	128
Chapter 7 Takeaways	132
Reflection	132

CHAPTER 8
Designing Digital Literacy Experiences

Designing Digital Literacy Instruction	134
Designing Digital Literacy Guide	137
References	138
Index	145

Introduction

All students need digital literacy skills to be responsible, participatory, and literate in school and society; however, teaching digital literacy can be challenging for teachers who have many other content standards they must address. Yet, the effort is worthwhile, because students with digital literacy can spend more time demonstrating mastery of content and engaging in a higher level of learning.

So, how do teachers improve students' digital literacy without a formal digital literacy curriculum? *Digital Literacy Made Simple: Strategies for Building Skills Across the Curriculum* explores the ways in which K–12 teachers can take small actions to teach digital literacy skills throughout the day and across various content areas.

To include digital literacy in classes without disrupting the curriculum, we propose that teachers weave digital literacy throughout instruction. With the addition of simple strategies, teachers can integrate, model, mentor, and build a learning culture and create digital experiences to improve students' digital literacy skills and habits in small ways throughout the day. Using practical examples that all teachers can implement immediately, this book is a useful guide for any teacher working to encourage digital literacy in their students.

What exactly do we mean by *digital literacy*? The term encompasses skills and ways of thinking related to the use of technology, including the competence to communicate, evaluate information, navigate websites, interpret digital information, and understand why all these skills are important. Supporting student growth in this vital area can be as simple as:

- Providing students with an opportunity to use technology
- Encouraging curiosity by modeling an information search to find the answer to a question
- Using think-aloud strategies to explain what makes a source credible
- Explaining relevant terms of use for students when using a technology in class
- Asking questions that prompt students to reflect on their understanding of information

What's in This Book

In *Digital Literacy Made Simple*, we'll expand on these ideas and introduce you to the Four Corners Framework, which consists of strategies for integration, culture, modeling, and mentoring. Using the Four Corners Framework, we'll frame teaching digital literacy around the technical skills and ways of thinking related to the use of technology, so you can help your students grow their skills too. The four parts of the Four Corners Framework are the central organizing structure for this book. Throughout the book, you'll learn creative and innovative strategies for integrating digital literacy into your curriculum—all while addressing the ISTE Standards for Educators.

Each chapter begins by highlighting the ISTE Standards it addresses and ends with a summary of key takeaways and reflection questions that will help you relate what you've learned to your own classroom. After discussing some of the research and science behind the Framework in Chapters 1 and 2, we'll dive deeper into each corner of the Framework in Chapters 3 through 6. The final two chapters will help you put what you've learned to work: Chapter 7 focuses on case studies of educators in various grade levels who share how they simply integrated digital literacy into their content areas. Chapter 8 contains a lesson plan template that will help you identify your own opportunities for increasing digital literacy for your students.

Whom This Book Is For

Digital Literacy Made Simple is for teachers who want to foster digital literacy skills in their students. Teachers are pressed for time and have many responsibilities throughout the day, so taking time to teach stand-alone lessons on digital literacy may not always be possible. We're here to tell you that you don't need to carve out a large chunk of your day—but you can make minutes count by incorporating the simple strategies of the Four Corners Framework throughout your day.

We hope you find this book practical and inspiring.

—Jenna and Lauren

CHAPTER 1
Understanding Digital Literacy for Your Classroom

KEY ISTE STANDARDS

This chapter addresses several ISTE Standard for Educators:

- Learner 2.1.a, 2.1.c
- Citizen 2.3.b
- Designer 2.5.a, 2.5.c

By the end of this chapter, you will:

- Define digital literacy.
- Name the core elements of digital literacy.
- Identify where digital literacy fits in schools.
- Describe a digitally literate student and a digitally literate teacher.

Digital Literacy Defined

What do you think of when you think of digital literacy? Ask someone not in education, and they may say that digital literacy is the technical ability to operate a mobile device or computer. If you ask ChatGPT what makes someone digitally literate, the response might be the ability to code and understand cybersecurity. However, when you ask someone in education, depending on the background of the educator, their definition of digital literacy may describe the skills needed to be digitally literate in that field. For example, a historian might say that managing one's online identity is a very important digital literacy skill (Denbo, 2016), as this creates a historical record of a person's history. A school librarian may say that digital literacy is being able to critically evaluate and find information online.

All of these interpretations of digital literacy are correct. Digital literacy is a broad and varied concept—and even expert definitions vary slightly. Mattson (2017) explained that while there are many digital literacy definitions, there are three commonly agreed-upon competencies:

> 1) the ability to decipher meaning from a variety of contexts including audio, images, and video; 2) the ability to match medium, purpose, and audience when communicating; and 3) the ability to locate, analyze, and use reliable sources of information online. (p. 94)

Teaching digital literacy is not a new concern for educators, but technology changes rapidly. Not only must educators learn to teach with technology, they must also adapt to emerging critical digital literacy skills that come with unlocking new technologies. Even though the skills we teach are evolving, digital literacy as a concept is rooted in one ultimate goal: lifelong learning. In 1997, Glister defined digital literacy as:

> a set of skills to access the internet, find, manage, and edit digital information; join in communications, and otherwise engage with an online information and communication network. Digital literacy is the ability to properly use and evaluate digital resources, tools, and services, and apply it to lifelong learning processes. (p. 220)

The ISTE Standards, while designed for use of technology in teaching and learning, support development of digital literacy skills. Within indicator b of Educator Standard 2.3, Citizen, ISTE defines digital literacy as "being able to use technologies effectively and being able to effectively discover, analyze, create and communicate information using digital tools and resources" (2017).

And finally, in a previous work, we defined digital literacy as "the ability to evaluate and critique information that is created and shared in digital mediums. To be digitally literate, persons must develop mental habits to adjust to new digital tools and content" (Hays & Kammer, 2021a, p. 2).

Notice the two parts to our definition. These are echoed in other definitions (Peng & Yu, 2022), but we want to be explicit about their use in K–12 contexts. The first part is an ability to navigate, create, and share, essentially an expertise in hardware and software. A digitally literate person is *not* an expert in everything–and they certainly do not need to be able to write code (though they might have that skill set)—but a digitally literate person also knows where their abilities with technology begin and end. They know to seek help from someone with more expertise than them, and their level of expertise may not be the same across all digital skills. While someone may be an expert at internet searching, they could still be developing literacy with creating slide presentations. Just as with all areas of literacy, digital literacy is not fixed; it is an area of knowledge where one can continually grow (see Table 1.1).

The second part of the definition has to do with *mental habits*: ways of thinking and acting that are automatic to a person based on signals they receive. An example of a digital literacy mental habit is to automatically restart your device when a program is not responding. Or, maybe you take a quick glance at the name of the online news source when you are reading an article on social media. We will explore these in more detail later in this chapter, but for now it is also useful to note that ways of thinking related to digital literacy were highlighted by Gilster (1997). Gilster wrote that digital literacy is the "the ability to understand" (p. 220) which emphasizes a mental component (Audrin & Audrin, 2022). Skills and mental habits are both necessary for digital literacy.

We would also like to point out that there is a difference between functional digital literacy and critical digital literacy (Polizzi, 2020). *Functional digital literacy* refers to the practical, technical skills needed to operate and use a technology, which can include using technology to create, navigate, or communicate. *Critical digital literacy* refers to the ability to evaluate digital information for trustworthiness, bias, and accuracy. For example, in the functional dimension, students know how to use a spreadsheet to create a visual representation of data. In the critical dimension, students know how to analyze the spreadsheet data in a visual representation to interpret and make meaning of the results, as well as understand where the data came from. The broad term of *digital literacy* encompasses both the functional and critical dimension and is not limited to just one (Figure 1.1).

FIGURE 1.1
The digital literacy model

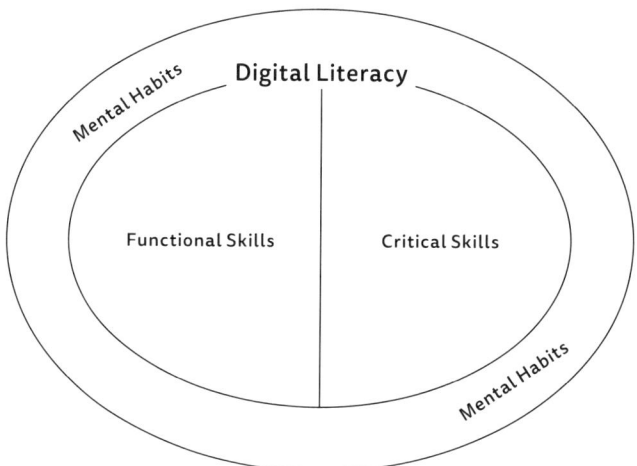

TABLE 1.1 What Is Digital Literacy?

DIGITAL LITERACY IS...	DIGITAL LITERACY IS NOT...
A life skill that is learned, continuously growing and evolving.	Assumed for students born in the digital age.
Using technology for thinking critically, communicating, evaluating information, and creating.	Only about functionality.
Integrated into all areas of living, learning, and productivity.	A separate skill.
A mindset that includes awareness of the ever-changing ways in which we access, manage, understand, and evaluate information.	A fixed mindset
The ability to use technology and adjust to new hardware and software.	Expertise in one technological area.

The Difference Between Digital Literacy and Digital Citizenship

Digital literacy and digital citizenship are very closely related. In fact, the two exist in tandem. A *digital citizen* is defined as someone who participates in the digital ecosystem and is therefore expected to engage in appropriate and responsible behavior when using technology. Because digital literacy involves understanding the digital world, some level of digital literacy must be present to be a digital citizen. In this book, we consider digital activity to include both elements of digital literacy and digital citizenship. While digital citizenship focuses more on behaviors (i.e., being a citizen of the digital world) when using technology, digital literacy focuses more on how to access, use, and understand the information processes when using technology. Digital literacy also includes the knowledge of how to use digital resources and the ability to use them well.

What Research Says

Digital literacy is a topic widely discussed in research literature and that continues to evolve among researchers and educators. Because a great deal of debate about digital literacy, its specific terminology, and how it manifests still abounds (Audrin & Audrin, 2022; Peng & Yu, 2022; Pangrazio et al., 2020), literature about the subject is fragmented, which is frustrating for educators. When authors and researchers are not consistent about digital literacy definitions and terms, teachers have a hard time knowing what to teach. Therefore, we are going to do our best to be clear about our meanings and terms before we jump into offering advice you can use in the classroom.

List (2019) describes three ways digital literacy researchers define digital literacy.

- One view of digital literacy that made its way into popular culture is the idea of a *digital native* (Prensky, 2001). According to Prensky (2001), "Our students today are all 'native speakers' of the digital language of computers, videos games, and the Internet…. Digital immigrants typically have very little appreciation for these new skills that the natives have acquired and perfected through years of interaction and practice" (pp. 3–4). However, this idea has been largely discredited by researchers (Bennet et al., 2008; Kennedy et al., 2008). Today's students know what interests them and are not naturally more digitally literate than others. Everyone must learn.

- Other researchers describe digital literacy as a set of skills (Eshet, 2004; Gilster, 1997), which is part of how we define digital literacy. These skills may involve communication, creation, or navigating.

- The third way List described the definition of digital literacy is through sociocultural perspectives. "Sociocultural perspectives are ones that emphasize the literacy aspects of digital literacy and, therefore, view digital literacy as connected to students' meaningful participation in a variety of online communities" (List, 2019, p. 148). In other words, digital literacy is shaped by individuals' engagement with digital environments. For example, a student may be engaged with technology related to being a student, but at home, they are engaged with technology for play or communicating with family and friends. Additionally, individuals must participate in the digital world to understand the context in which information is created and shared.

Within the English-speaking literature, Pangrazio et al. (2020) also emphasize different ways digital literacy is seen by researchers. In their work, they focus on how digital literacy is a concept that concerns many in society, but it is also an educational initiative. Finally, they argue that digital literacy has become too broad. Because it covers many areas, the term *digital literacy* can easily be confused with other terms such as *information literacy* and *media literacy*.

Because the research makes it apparent that digital literacy is a concept that is not always clear, we are going to strive to break it down into core elements so that digital literacy practices can be mapped for inclusion in curriculum. This involves identifying where student learning would benefit from increased understanding of technology. For example, before students can produce, publish, or cite sources, they need to have word processing skills. Before students can create graphic representations, they need to understand how to use spreadsheets. What we want you to keep in mind, though, is that we see digital literacy as a "life skill"—one we feel we must be teaching from an early age—that continues through adulthood (Tinmaz et al., 2022a).

Digital Natives

In his 2001 book *Digital Natives, Digital Immigrants*, Prensky popularized the idea that students born into a world saturated with technology are "all 'native speakers' of the digital language of computers, video games, and the internet" (p. 1). This work sent the message to educators that students knew how to use technology so there was no reason to teach them.

Subsequent research, however, has not supported this conclusion (Bennet et al., 2008; Kennedy et al., 2008; Kirschner & De Bruyckere, 2017). While students born in the digital age may have been exposed more to technology, they are more comfortable with some technology (like social media or video platforms) than others (like coding, cybersecurity, hardware maintenance or repair, or understanding the differences in information sources). Expertise, or even familiarity, in one area cannot be extrapolated to expertise in all, so students need to be supported when learning to use technology. Not teaching students needed skills they will use as citizens and in the workplace exacerbates social inequalities (OCED & Eynon, 2020).

The Core Elements of Digital Literacy

Based on the way others have defined and described digital literacy, and as we have worked with digital literacy ourselves, we have determined that we believe digital literacy encompasses both skills and mental habits. In other words, *a digitally literate person is someone who can effectively navigate a digital world and can think effectively about digital information and digital systems.*

What are the skills that a person needs to be digitally literate? Some examples include:

- How to navigate websites
- How to troubleshoot basic technology problems
- How to use computer programs, apps, and mobile devices
- How to find information when they do not know how to do something
- How to communicate in digital environments

Also, according to ISTE (**getdigitalskills.org**), the key skills digitally literate learners need are the ability to:

- **Locate information:** Use digital technology to effectively search for relevant and reliable information sources.
- **Evaluate sources:** Analyze sources of digital information for credibility, bias, and influence.
- **Interpret information:** Determine meaning from various digital sources that represent multiple perspectives.
- **Express ideas:** Create digital content to express themselves and voice their ideas.
- **Communicate with others:** Safely and responsibly collaborate with and learn from others online, including those who think differently than them.
- **Navigate technology ecosystems:** Be aware that their online actions influence their digital landscape, leave a trail, and impact their privacy.

So far we've discussed skills needed for successfully navigating the digital world, but a digitially literate person also needs to think effectively about digital information and systems; they need certain habits of mind. The Institute for Habits of Mind (2022) defines these mental habits as "dispositions or thinking behaviors that are desirable attributes for learning and living productively in a complex world" (para. 1), while Plymouth State University (2023) describes habits of mind as "a usual way of thinking, a way of engaging with the everyday world" (para. 3).

What makes up habits of mind? According to Costa (n.d.) habits of mind involve values, inclinations, sensitivities, capabilities, and commitments. As Costa (n.d.) described:

> *Employing "Habits of Mind" requires a composite of many skills, attitudes, cues, past experiences, and proclivities. It means that we value one pattern of thinking over another and therefore it implies choice making about which pattern should be employed at this time. It includes alertness to the contextual cues that signal this as an appropriate time and circumstance in which the employment of this pattern would be useful. It requires a level of skillfulness to employ and carry through the behaviors effectively over time. It suggests that because of each experience in which these behaviors were employed, the effects of their use are reflected upon, evaluated, modified and carried forth to future applications. (para. 3)*

Plymouth State University describes four specific habits of mind that they seek to cultivate: purposeful communication, problem-solving, integrative perspective, and self-regulated learning. The Institute of Habits of Mind has a slightly longer list, as Figure 1.2 shows.

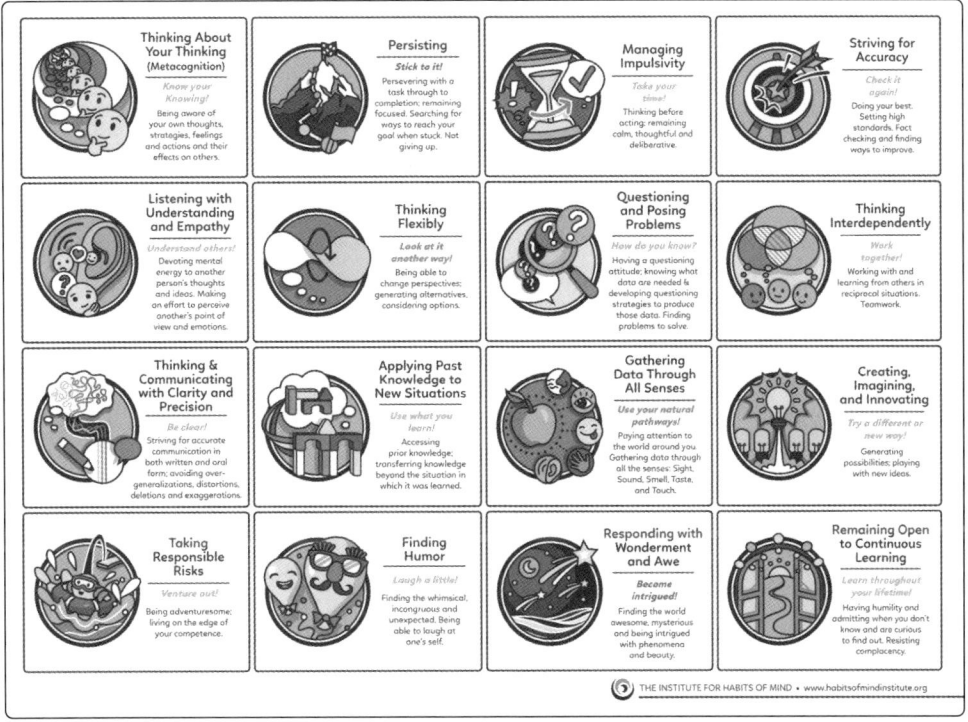

FIGURE 1.2 The habits of mind defined by the Institute for Habits of Mind. Image courtesy of the Institute for Habits of Mind, habitsofmindinstitute.org.

Of the Institite's 16 habits, persisting, striving for accuracy, and thinking interdependently are all familiar habits to teachers; we want to see them in students and encourage them regularly. But, have you thought about the importance of responding with wonderment and awe or finding humor in the learning process? Those two were a surprise to us! Upon reflection, however, we realized that, of course, they are important mental habits for learning. Including elements of humor and encouraging wonderment can engage students and add a positive perspective that can motivate them. Without humor and wonderment, how can we expect students to strive for more?

Misinformation and Digital Literacy

There is a close relationship between misinformation and digital literacy. In fact, the rise of misinformation goes hand in hand with interest in the policy and practice of digital literacy. Misinformation (defined as information that is not complete) and disinformation (defined as information meant to mislead) are pervasive online and can be discussed in terms of credibility, trustworthiness, and deception, and can also lead to discussions about the motivations behind information-sharing (Cooke, 2018). It has been theorized that people fall for misinformation and disinformation because they lack digital literacy skills, making them more susceptible to believing falsehoods. However, Sirlin et al. (2021) found that *sharing* misinformation and *believing* misinformation are two different things: People will share misinformation because they don't take the time to investigate the source.

In this book, we focus on developing the habits of mind needed to be digitally literate, rather than discerning between real and fake information. This includes habits that involve considering motivation behind information and pausing to consider what is known about the information before sharing.

Learning about habits of mind, changed our way of thinking about digital literacy, and we believe that mental habits relate to how we want people to think about digital literacy. We all need to have certain ways of thinking to be digitally literate.

So, let's bring this all together and talk about the habits of mind needed for digital literacy. Students in K–12 need to start learning four habits of mind:

- **Evaluation skills:** Be able to assess the quality of both hardware and software to determine what will meet needs. Evaluation skills also involve being able to critique digital information. This is particularly important with the pervasiveness of misinformation and disinformation online.
- **Problem solving:** Involves technical expertise. Individuals who are digitally literate need to be able to solve hardware and software problems. They also need to be able to think through content problems and solve them with digital tools.

- **Lifelong learning:** Technology changes rapidly, and it is important to stay current on new tools, resources, and ways of understanding how content is generated online. This is sometimes described as a *growth mindset*, which includes being open to learning and developing for improvement.
- **Situational understanding:** Involves the ability to understand digital needs and digital information in various contexts.

The Problem of Digital Literacy in Schools

The problem of digital literacy in schools is complex and requires that schools address bigger issues such as access and teacher training, while also focusing on developing digital literacy skills in the classroom. In addition, teachers are faced with the challenge of ensuring that students have the necessary skills and knowledge to effectively use digital technologies (which are increasingly integrated into education) for learning.

The problem of access, often referred to as the *digital divide*, relates to the gap in access to technology and internet connectivity between students from different socio-economic backgrounds (Bennett et al., 2008). Students from low-income families or those attending schools in rural or remote areas may not have the same access to technology as their more affluent or urban peers, which can limit their ability to develop digital literacy skills.

Another challenge is that teaching digital literacy requires teachers to be trained on using technology, teaching with technology, and students' use of technology. Many teachers may not have the necessary training or resources to effectively integrate technology into their lessons, which can limit students' exposure to digital tools, their application for learning, and hinder their development of digital literacy skills.

Furthermore, historically there has been a focus on teaching students how to use specific tools or software, rather than developing broader digital literacy skills such as critical thinking, problem-solving, and information literacy. And, as we have stated earlier, students often lack the mental habits needed to develop digital literacy within content areas. Without these skills, students may struggle to navigate the vast amounts of information available online and to evaluate the credibility and accuracy of sources.

To foster digital literacy skills in students, we need to step back and think through the different ways we can teach and encourage digital literacy. There are various frameworks for integrating technology into teaching, such as TPACK (Mishra & Koehler, 2006), SAMR (Puentedura, 2006), and PIC-RAT (Ottenbreit-Leftwich & Kimmon, 2018), but no framework currently exists that looks at what educators can do to specifically develop digital literacy in their students. We aim to fill that gap with the content of this book!

Teaching Digital Literacy in Schools

Without an established framework for teaching digital literacy, we sought to develop one. Developing a teaching framework involves reflection, research, analysis, and experimentation. We researched the various models and theories related to teaching technology, as well as existing standards (like the ISTE Standards for Educators), and observed teachers using different strategies to teach digital literacy. While this is an ongoing process and all teaching frameworks should undergo continuous reflection and adaptation, the framework we arrived at is called The Four Corners Framework (Figure 1.3) and consists of four parts:

- Integration
- Culture
- Modeling
- Mentorship

FIGURE 1.3
The Four Corners Framework for developing digital literacy in students

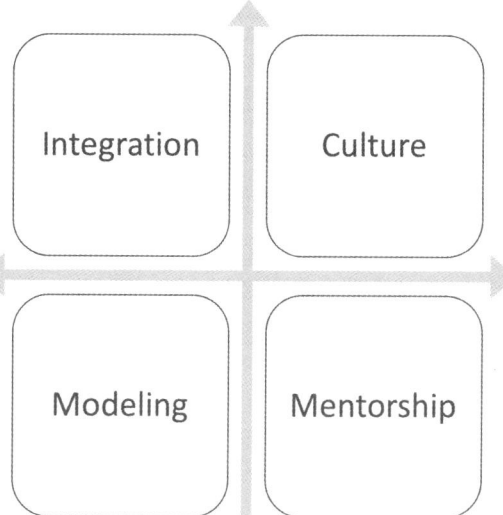

The sections that follow introduce the key considerations needed at each corner of the Framework, then we'll dive into deeper detail in upcoming chapters. We have organized the strategies in this book into four overarching teaching strategies that include integrating experiences, working within a learning culture, modeling, and mentoring.

Integration

First, teachers integrate digital literacy within content to promote habits of mind by aligning pedagogy with such habits as thinking, listening, communicating clearly, creating questioning, or finding humor. To do so, we need to be thoughtful about the pedagogy we select and what mental processes it is encouraging in students. We must look for gaps in digital literacy and find creative solutions to address these within the context of student instruction.

In Chapter 3, we will talk about designing integrated experiences to teach digital literacy. An integrated learning experience is one that is not separate from other learning objectives but is instead integrated into existing instruction to enhance the outcomes. These are often discovered when a teacher identifies a gap in digital literacy skills.

Culture

Second, teachers develop a culture of digital literacy and work within the school culture already available. This involves collaborating, coordinating, and coteaching to organize efforts, while also learning from each other. In Chapter 4, we will talk about developing a culture of digital literacy as a simple strategy. This involves understanding how the people in your own environment are teaching digital literacy and knowing when to work with them. It also recognizes that what happens in one classroom can be continued in other learning spaces.

Modeling

Third, teachers model the mental habits they want students to possess. In this case, modeling also means discussing the mental habits out loud and helping students understand our thought process. Explaining how we come to decisions, how we evaluate content, how we develop an interest in lifelong learning, how we solve problems, and so on helps students develop these mental habits for themselves. One reason mental habits can be challenging to develop is that they are hidden.

Some students will naturally possess some of the habits of mind, others will pick up on them over time because they are invested in the courses and content, and others will need more explicit instruction.

In addition to modeling the mental habits of a digitally literate person, teachers should model the practices as well. Students can learn digital literacy practices, such as communicating online, navigating digital infrastructure (i.e., websites), and searching for information by watching their teacher do those things. In Chapter 5, we will talk about using modeling to teach digital literacy. Modeling involves demonstrating how to do something, but it can also involve presenting and sharing models of a process or strategy. With digital literacy, this can involve teacher modeling of proper care of devices, or it can involve modeling how to use the features of a technology.

Mentorship

Fourth, learning from others is a reciprocal and collaborative experience that can drive personal growth and build relationships. Teachers need opportunities to work with mentors to learn how to incorporate digital literacy in their classrooms. Mentoring may come from veteran teachers or develop from new teachers sharing their ideas. Digital literacy is a skill that any teacher can be an expert in. Students can also be involved in mentoring, by mentoring each other and sometimes even mentoring teachers! Mentoring is a strategy that is often associated with collaborative support. This support is critical for learning about new technologies and can be optimized to both learn and teach simple strategies. In Chapter 6, we will talk about how mentorship, both formal and informal, can be a gift between two people who are learning about new technologies.

A Portrait of a Digitally Literate Teacher

For teachers to be able to implement simple strategies that support students in growing their digital literacy skills, they need to have digital literacy skills themselves. Without strong digital literacy skills of their own, teachers cannot integrate these skills, model them, mentor students in digital literacy, or develop a culture where digital literacy is a focus. So, let's consider a portrait of a digitally literate teacher.

Taylor has been teaching high school social studies for eight years. Her day starts with checking her email and reviewing her lesson plans. Each day she brings in a few current event news articles to use as a bell activity. She quickly jumps to sites she knows are reliable based on criteria she and her teammates determined. When Taylor accesses one site, she notices that the interface has changed. She takes a moment to orient herself to the updated site and can find what she needs because she understands how news sites are organized. On the site, she reads the articles to identify bias and influence, asking questions like "Who wrote this? What was their purpose in writing this? What do others say about it?" It is important for her to know what is in each article before she gives them to her students.

After Taylor selects current event articles, she creates a short video on the events discussed in the articles. She does this to model for students how to clearly communicate ideas in video form.

After she is ready for the day, she messages another teacher about a collaborative presentation they are developing for a teacher in-service. She makes a few notes about how they are collaborating so she can share the strategies with her students later in the day as they work on group projects. Finally, before the bell rings and students enter her room, she makes sure she is logged out of any sites that she does not want open and that her camera is off.

Maybe you are already doing some of these things—see, you're on the right track! Keep trying, and let's talk about moving to the next level!

The End Game: A Portrait of a Digitally Literate Student

Digitally literate teachers develop digitally literate students. Once we have implemented digital literacy in our school culture and pedagogy, and we provide opportunities for modeling and mentoring of digital literacy skills and mental habits, we are on our way to students becoming digitally literate. But, what does that destination look like? If you know the end goal, getting there will be easier. Consider this portrait of a digitally literate student as an opportunity to practice backwards design.

Jordan is in eleventh grade. Recently, he has been receiving electronic communication from colleges and is trying to decide what his next steps are going to be. Jordan has considered several colleges and universities. These options have led him to do a lot of research online. Jordan is also paying close attention to the communication he receives.

Jordan has spent time on different schools' websites but knows that each school is marketing themselves. Therefore, he uses the information from the websites to determine curricular offerings and cost. He can navigate the websites and find this information. When he has not been able to locate a piece of information that is important to him, he can locate the contact information for his admissions counselor and email, call, or text with questions. Jordan can check the admission system to know which email address the counselor will use to contact him and follow his application through the different stages. Jordan knows which form of communication to use for different questions.

Additionally, Jordan tries to decipher the implicit focus of the school when reviewing school websites. When reviewing school websites, Jordan asks himself questions such as: What is the school emphasizing (e.g., sports, academics, location, or something else)? Who is represented in the site images? What information is critical to know (application process, deadlines, costs)?

When questions remain, Jordan knows he can search social media to see what current students are discussing. However, he is cautious and recognizes that social media is only a one-dimensional view of a student's college experience. Jordan is willing to meet people in-person and have conversations as well.

Overall, Jordan feels confident about his next steps. Even though he is undecided about the future and nervous about leaving behind established relationships, he has been preparing for this and feels ready. Jordan learned early on the importance of digital content and while he enjoys engaging online, he is also aware of his online actions. He does not feel that negative digital content will follow him to college and beyond. Instead, Jordan knows he can confidently move forward.

Chapter 1 Takeaways

In this section, the important takeaways from the chapter are paired with the ISTE Standards for Educators that inform them.

- Digital literacy is composed of both a set of skills and habits of mind. Teachers can learn about these theories and definitions to support their practice (Learner 2.1.c).
- To teach digital literacy, teachers can support students by designing innovative digital learning experiences (Designer 2.5.c):
  - Develop a culture of digital literacy.
  - Integrate digital literacy with content.
  - Model the mental habits of digital literacy.
  - Create mentorship opportunities for fellow educators and students.
- Developing portraits of digitally literate teachers and students provides you with the opportunity to work backwards and design curriculum and a school environment that moves students toward digital literacy, while also accomodating their differences and needs. You may use the portraits in this book as is or modify them (Designer 2.5.a).

Reflection

Before moving on, take some time to consider how the ideas in Chapter 1 apply within your context using the questions below.

- What are areas of digital literacy strengths in your school?
- Where do you see digital literacy opportunities in your school?
- What digital literacy skills do you want to cultivate in your students?
- What digital literacy habits of mind do you want to cultivate in your students?
- Which habits of mind do you see promoted in your school?

CHAPTER 2
Digital Literacy as a Simple Strategy

KEY ISTE STANDARDS

This chapter addresses several ISTE Standards for Educators:

- Learner 2.1.c
- Collaborator 2.4.a
- Designer 2.5.c
- Facilitator 2.6.b

By the end of this chapter, you will:

- Understand the impact of a simple strategy for teaching digital literacy.
- Understand how the science of learning supports the use of simple strategies in teaching.
- Start to view yourself as an architect of learning digital literacy in the modern classroom, embracing the flexibility of integrating digital literacy into practice.
- Understand the theory- and research-based rationales for incorporating simple strategies into teaching.

Teaching Digital Literacy Simply

Though students use technology regularly and are adept when using mobile devices, gaming and social media, digital literacy is not necessarily discovered while engaging in these activities.

We propose that teaching digital literacy can be done effectively with simple strategies. Maybe you have heard the term *small teaching* thrown around. The small teaching movement has been underway since 2016 and is a strategy for teaching material in small increments in your classroom. What does that really involve? Simply put, James Lang (2021) described small teaching as any combination of short modifications to teaching practice. Small teaching can include brief (five- to ten-minute) activities, one-time interventions, or small modifications in curriculum design. Using incremental approaches in an already designed curriculum was found to raise student performance, improve knowledge retention, and develop lasting skills. This book approaches teaching digital literacy within the context of using minimal techniques, while also focusing on strategies that can be integrated not only in teaching, but also the broader school environment as well. Our goal for approaching digital literacy this way is so that simple strategies can be incorporated where they will have the most impact without overburdening any one person.

The Science Behind Simple Strategies for Digital Literacy

When we began research for this book, we discovered that many teachers did not think they taught digital literacy. Some said that only the technology specialist or the school librarian taught digital literacy in their school. The more we probed, however, the more we found that teachers were indeed aware of the affordances that technology, and the ability to use it for learning, brought to their students, which is the start of teaching digital literacy. Many teachers are using technology designed with the theories of learning science in mind. For example, a teacher who uses Kahoot! (kahoot.com), a learning game that allows students to guess the right answer and compete with others, is integrating the following ideas from learning science:

- **Retrieval practice.** Many teachers create Kahoot! questions that enable students to use memory to retrieve what they know. Retrieving is the process of recalling information and can be considered a memory exercise. Retrieving is most commonly practiced in test-taking and is sometimes called the "testing effect" because tests often require students to pull from what they know (Nunes & Karpicke, 2015). Agarwal et al. (2020) explained that the practice of retrieval is the act of getting information out (as opposed to bringing new information in).

- **Predicting.** Some teachers create Kahoot! questions that ask students to think about what might happen. Predicting is a skill that involves forecasting what is believed will occur in the future (Predicting, n.d., para. 2). When a student creates a prediction, they are drawing on prior knowledge, experiences, observations, and research. Brod (2021) explained that predicting (whether the prediction is correct or incorrect) boosts learning because it increases the retention of learned material, by allowing students to think about what may be correct, but also engaging them when finding out the correct answer.

However, relying on memory or making predictions does not necessarily teach digital literacy. When teachers use more aligned ideas from learning science, and even integrate them into an activity like a Kahoot! game, students benefit more and can develop skills that can prepare them to be more digitally literate. Here are some other ideas from learning science that you can easily integrate into teaching to support development of digital literacy:

- **Engagement.** Engaged learning is one the main reasons that teachers use technology for teaching. However, Bergdahl et al. (2018) suggested that it is not the educational technology alone that engages students, but the invisible learning process that happens when using a technology for learning. For example, peer modeling (students showing each other how and what they did) and teacher feedback (teachers providing suggestions and guidance to students while they are making decisions) while participating in an online game may be more effective than playing the game alone.

- **Visibility.** The concept of visibility was first described by John Hattie (2009) as a strategy that suggests that learning becomes visible when the teacher reflects on their own teaching and also allows students to become their own teachers. Using a technology like Kahoot! makes learning more visible to the teacher and students when students have the opportunity to think and discuss questions as they are given. Some teachers may allow students to create questions for a kahoot, which adds another element of critical thinking to the activity. Hattie (2023) found that when students are able to discuss together in class to solve problems, their learning doubles.

- **Connections to prior knowledge.** Miller (2022) wrote that connecting new information to prior knowledge is an important part of learning. Information that does not fit within our existing understanding is more easily forgotten. Therefore, when introducing new technologies, teachers can offer a brief explanation of how the technology is like, or not like, a tool that students have used before. This will help connect new information to prior knowledge. Students can also think more about the tool using prior knowledge. Using the example of Kahoot!, teachers can take time to reflect on the game, including asking students to think about how this game is made possible because all students have their own devices and a good wireless network, and that it combines social networking and gaming into one experience.
- **Personal relevance.** Miller (2022) also wrote about the importance of personal relevance for learning. Students learn better when they understand why the information matters to them. With digital literacy, students may feel they are already very knowledgeable about technology, but there are many things they will not know and will need to know. To make digital literacy relevant, teachers can share stories of their own technology use, give examples of how individuals in the workforce use technology, or ask students to develop their own digital literacy goals to meet throughout the class.

For example, Adrienne Smith (2018) in *Edtech for the K–12 Classroom* suggested that one way to teach the skills of analyzing and evaluating would be for teachers to shift their role to allow opportunities for controversy or to let students choose the content. This not only increases visibility, but also increases opportunities for critical thinking. One reason that class discussions are so effective is that the student is doing the thinking, rather than the teacher. And the thinking is happening across students, rather than one student bearing the weight of doing all the thinking, which we know leads to cognitive overload. Sweller (2020) refers to this as *cognitive load theory*, suggesting that working memory is limited and overloading it reduces the effectiveness of both working and long-term memory. Technology for learning can play an important role in reducing cognitive load; however, it is important that schools develop digital literacy in both teachers and students so that there is an understanding of the affordances that are offered by each tool to better understand how technology supports learning (Ng, 2011).

Digital Literacy Within the Learning System

One of the main takeaways from this book is that digital literacy is not taught in a single moment or lesson, but is integrated more fully throughout small, simple practices and across different learning communities to create a more robust culture of digital literacy. In fact, there are no agreed upon standards of digital literacy. Likewise, there are very few policies related to digital literacy, and it is taught with a wide variety of curriculum (if at all). Teachers benefit when their students have increased digital literacy, however, because the technology-enabled classroom runs more smoothly and students produce better quality of work.

Teachers may be surprised to learn that effective teaching and learning strategies for digital literacy are actually the same ones that many teachers have been using every day since their teacher education programs. For example, science teachers often model each step in a lab before asking students to do it. These same strategies can be applied to teach digital literacy. The incredible thing about using simple strategies to teach digital literacy is their flexibility. Digital literacy looks different based on each individual classroom, the subject taught, the school, students, and even a teacher's own digital literacy. Students also come to class with differing digital abilities, learned throughout their own experiences in the world. We like to think about digital literacy as part of a system (Figure 2.1), with the school strategies and infrastructure on one end, and the students' own personal experiences on the other end. Teachers prepare students for any combination of these activities so that students are successful when using technology for academics or personal pursuits!

FIGURE 2.1
Students are influenced by a variety of factors that have the potential to work together to develop their digital literacy.

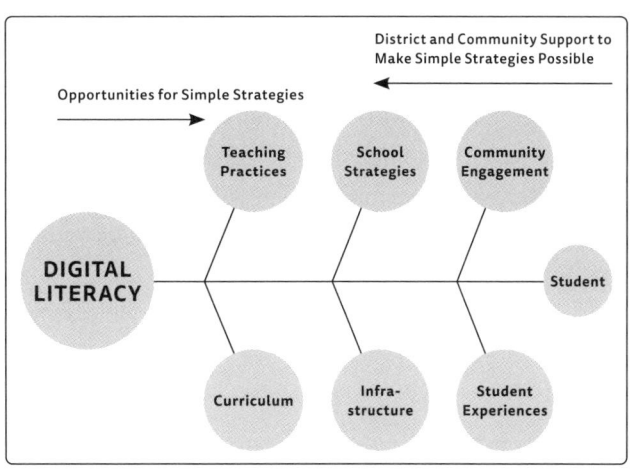

Throughout this system are formally defined components of digital literacy, ranging from school-sponsored digital literacy initiatives to the personal experiences students have when learning to use technology at home and in their community. Teachers have an opportunity to use their own teaching practices, within the boundaries of their curriculum, the infrastructure of the school, and school strategies, to improve students' digital literacy. While digital literacy should start in the school, the good news is that students have opportunities for learning digital literacy outside of the classroom, taking the burden off teachers!

Let's look more closely at each of the influences on digital literacy, starting with the experiences that an individual student may have, experiences that make the student unique. While one **student's experience** with technology at home may include high speed internet access for use on personal computers with the latest operating system, another student may rely on accessing the internet with a mobile phone that has limited data. Either student may also experience successes from using this technology, as well as technical difficulties and distractions.

The extent of **community engagement** in technology efforts can also impact a student's digital literacy. For example, a community initiative to integrate technology into social spaces outside of home, work, or school (also referred to as *third spaces*) can increase opportunities for using digital literacy, such as providing the digital environment needed to begin to engage in digital learning, communications, creation, and other digital practices (McDougall et al., 2018). These spaces can include public libraries, community centers, coffee shops, after-school programs, and other local initiatives.

School strategies for supporting digital literacy will include a variety of training, policies, and school-wide initiatives designed to develop students' digital literacy and technological awareness. This may include digital literacy, digital citizenship, or computer use. Training for parents related to using school-provided technology or digital literacy issues may also occur during open house night, special programming or through correspondence (like email or newsletters).

The **infrastructure** that supports digital literacy includes the broadband network, the equipment, access points, training for staff, and opportunities to use technology throughout the educational space. An infrastructure which supports digital literacy can improve outcomes for students, including the most vulnerable and excluded students (Bandura & Méndez Leal, 2022).

Many states use updated **curriculum** in schools that includes digital-age skills. For example, the K–5 English Language Arts (ELA) Missouri Learning Standards (MLS) include a strand for digital and media literacy that intersects with learning comprehension and analysis of words, images, graphics, and other media (Missouri Department of Elementary and Secondary Education, 2016). Schools may also have a digital literacy curriculum that is created by the district; for example the 2022 Massachusetts Digital Literacy and Computer Science Curriculum (STEM Learning Design, 2022) aligns digital literacy with computer science. Or a school may adopt a digital literacy program like Ellipsis Education Computer Science Courses (**ellipsiseducation.com**) or the Keyboarding without Tears (**kwtears.com**) program to support students learning digital literacy for computer science.

The **teaching practices** used within a classroom to teach digital literacy are the foundation of this book. Teachers use strategies every day to engage students and promote learning. The way that digital literacy is incorporated into these strategies is critical for developing and reinforcing digital skills and habits of mind, particularly in relation to their use in academics. It is also often reliant on the curriculum, schools' strategies, and infrastructure. Stenger (2018) suggested that teaching practices include emphasizing the importance of critical thinking, use of social media for learning and collaborating, providing guidance for avoiding plagiarism, teaching students to manage their online identity and digital distractions, providing authentic contexts for practice, and encouraging students to move out of their comfort zone using freedom of choice and encouragement.

It is because of this system that simple strategies are likely to have an impact. A simple strategy is not intended to measure competence of digital literacy but is intended to provide students with more opportunities to use digital literacy and reinforce the application of digital literacy within the context of everyday activities.

Future Ready Schools (FRS) and Support for Digital Literacy

While adapted for this book, Figure 2.1 is based on research compiled for the Future Ready Schools (FRS) Framework, which describes approaches for school leadership teams to support digital learning in their districts (U.S. Department of Education, 2015). Teaching digital literacy is easier with support from the district. The FRS Framework explains that to build capacity for digital learning, school leaders need to provide:

- **Collaborative leadership.** School leaders commit to developing a vision around digital learning for the school, which includes the funding and the personnel to support it.
- **Personalized student learning.** School leaders commit to providing standards-aligned opportunities for students through personalized pathways. These are often made possible through robust digital tools, rich learning resources, and ongoing assessment of student progress and preference.
- **Robust infrastructure.** Digital learning is made possible through good bandwidth, wireless, technology equipment, and software with reliable technical support for both students and teachers.
- **Personalized professional learning.** Teachers need to continually learn and update their own digital skills and need opportunities for professional development and collaboration.

By signing the future-ready pledge, a school's administration and school leaders commit to ensuring the school is future ready. Once these things are in place, teachers have more support to focus on using technology in their classroom for teaching and learning. A future-ready school is committed to creating a culture of digital readiness!

The ISTE Standards and The Future Ready Librarians (FRL) Framework Crosswalk

Do you have a school librarian in your school? School librarians are experts in information, educational technology and love of reading. In addition, they often work with teachers and staff from all subjects areas and in all departments of the school. Recognizing the critical role that school librarians play in preparing learners, ISTE developed a crosswalk with the Future Ready Librarians (FRL) Framework. The FRL program is an adaptation of the Future Ready Schools (FRS) Framework and re-imagines ways in which librarians provide leadership within the areas of literacy, curriculum, instruction and assessment, personalized professional learning, robust infrastructure, budget and resources, community partnerships, data and privacy, use of space and time, and collaborative leadership. This adaptation of the FRS Framework demonstrates actionable ways for librarians to teach, lead and innovate within these areas.

The FRL Framework recognizes the library as an important school strategy to support digital initiatives. Figueroa (2018) explained that librarians can scan new trends in libraries to align with the priorities of the FRL's program. For example, librarians may offer 360-degree video as a resource in the library, as well as the technical training to prepare students to use it in their projects.

Collaboration with a school librarian to improve students' digital literacy is a simple strategy that works for many teachers who want to support digital literacy in their classroom. Ask your school librarian to teach a lesson to your students on crafting search terms or curating resources on a research topic. School librarians can also teach students about citing sources, evaluating information, and refining research topics.

Simple Ways to Include Digital Literacy

Although digital literacy initiatives will look different in every district, school, and classroom, we propose that teachers can easily include digital literacy into their existing instruction with simple instructional strategies that support what we know about learning. The examples that follow in this book include strategies that take ten minutes or less, with some not taking any additional time at all. For example, a school librarian in Missouri explained that when teaching students to save their files, like reports that they are writing, he takes a minute or two to explain to students that their Google Drive will store many files but does have limited space. He asks them to think about if a file needs to be saved and for how long. This very simple strategy, which does not distract from the main lesson being taught, takes less than a minute to teach students about an important digital literacy skill (information management) and is related to the work they are doing.

Examples of Simple Strategies

After all the discussion about the importance of simple strategies for teaching digital literacy, and why they work, you're probably wondering what a simple strategy looks like in the classroom. In Chapter 7, you will find case studies of how educators in different content areas and grade levels use simple strategies to teach digital literacy. For now, here are a few quick examples of teachers using simple strategies in the classroom, paired with the relevant ISTE Standards:

- In an elementary school, a first-grade teacher was teaching students about different genres during their ELA unit. In this classroom, students had access to Epic! (a digital library for kids 12 and under; **getepic.com**). The teacher had a brief consultation with each student to find out their interest in genres (biographies, animal stories, poems). Then the teacher created digital collections within Epic! curating books for students based on genre. The teacher found that students were interested in reading digital books in their preferred genre, but then also became interested in reading genres that other students were interested in. As the year went on, students also asked the teacher to make more digital collections and made recommendations of their own books to add to each genre. Through this example of instructors mentoring students, students developed an understanding of genre, digital curation, and information organization (Collaborator 2.4.b).

- A high school librarian was told that students in a social studies class were having trouble finding quality sources on school laptops for their research papers. The librarian visited the social studies class and provided a brief demo for students on one of the topics where the students were not finding sources. The demo showed students how they may not find anything in a Google search due to the topic for a variety of reasons (some content may be blocked by internet filters, some may not have full-text articles online, etc.), but searching the library database for that topic would provide an excellent body of sources to use. The demo included use of good search terms and how to use the built-in citation tools of the database. Students were able to visit the library during class or during open scheduling to get more help on their research. The collaboration between the teacher and the librarian is an example of building a learning culture to support digital literacy (Citizen 2.3.b).

- A middle school computer science teacher teaches introductory students to understand the new and complex language of computer science by showing them how to define and understand terms. Instead of telling students the definition of a word, however, he has students look up the word online using digital reference sources. Teaching vocabulary is not a separate part of the class, but is instead embedded into all classes, with students eventually becoming self-sufficient as they learn to use information resources to understand the meaning of the new terms they are learning. Through this example of a digital learning experience that was integrated into existing instruction, students developed an understanding of technical vocabulary and using information resources (Facilitator 2.6.d).

- A kindergarten teacher was having problems with student devices not being charged when they were needed. To solve this problem, she modeled to students how to plug in their devices when they were not in use. Each time the lesson using devices was over, she ended by modeling plugging in her device. By the middle of the semester, students were also plugging in their devices and bringing them back to school fully charged as well. Through this example of instructional modeling, students learned about proper care of devices (Collaborator 2.4.b).

- A seventh grade Language Arts teacher takes the first two minutes of each class period to show a word processing tip that will make writing and editing easier. The tip highlights keyboard shortcuts for common actions, like cut and paste or saving. For bell work, students are asked to keep a digital notebook where they make note of the tips and refer to them during assignments throughout the class. Through this example of modeling, students learned digital skills for productivity (Collaborator 2.4.b).

Chapter 2 Takeaways

In this section, the important takeaways from the chapter are paired with the ISTE Standards for Educators that inform them.

- A simple strategy is any combination of small, intentional lessons taught within existing instruction to further develop and support learning (Designer 2.5.c).

  Simple strategies are supported by the science of learning, which recognizes that learning occurs when learning conditions are met (Learner 2.1.c).

- Teaching digital literacy is not an isolated task. Students have opportunities to learn digital literacy throughout their whole educational experience, including their own personal experiences in their communities. The classroom teacher can enhance that experience (Collaborator 2.4.a).

- Simple strategies include finding and embracing everyday moments to teach digital literacy in ways that are natural and authentic. These can include utilizing a learning culture, integrated experiences, mentoring, and modeling (Facilitator 2.6.b).

Reflection

Before moving on, take some time to consider how the ideas in Chapter 2 apply within your context using the questions below.

- What simple strategies do you already use in your classroom?
- How are you supported by your school and district to teach digital learning? Are there new opportunities you may be able to leverage?
- What problems could you solve by incorporating digital literacy in simple ways in your classroom?

CHAPTER 3

Creating Integrated Digital Literacy Experiences

KEY ISTE STANDARDS

This chapter addresses several ISTE Standards for Educators:

- Learner 2.1.b, 2.1.c
- Citizen 2.3.a
- Designer 2.5.a

By the end of this chapter, you will:

- Recognize how digital literacy is integrated into content.
- Describe strategies you can use to create opportunities within existing lessons to teach digital literacy.
- Identify ways to integrate digital literacy into curriculum.

Where to Start?

This is the question that can be the hardest to answer. If you want to integrate digital literacy into your curriculum, where do you start? The key is to start small. Use simple strategies to integrate digital literacy into the curriculum. While digital literacy can be taught as a stand-alone lesson, it does not need to be, and may in fact lose some of its impact when it is separated from content. Instead, digital literacy can be integrated in simple ways into the instruction you're already providing in your classroom.

This is a similar approach to the one ISTE recommends for teaching digital citizenship. About digital citizenship, it has been said that "the idea now is for schools to have digital citizenship so well integrated, it's evident in every digital action by teachers and students" (Fingal, 2022, para. 2). We suggest that digital literacy should be taught in the same way. When a digital literacy curriculum is not available, the skills and habits of mind to become digitally literate should be integrated into the actions teachers and students take daily—in simple ways.

If you want to start with simple strategies that are integrated into the curriculum, what does this look like? Broadly, it breaks down into four actionable steps:

1. Start with yourself.
2. Emphasize digital literacy where it is already being used.
3. Identify areas where students have low digital competence.
4. Ask students to use digital literacy and teach it.

Let's take a closer look at each of these steps.

Start with Yourself

There are many times in our days as teachers that we are using digital literacy skills in the classroom, but we may not share that with students. When starting with yourself, start by making the digital literacy skills and habits of mind you are already using apparent to students. This is like modeling, which we will discuss in Chapter 5.

CONNECTIONS: ISTE STANDARDS

2.1 Learner. Educators continually imporove their practice by learning from and with others and exploring proven and promising practices that leverage technology to improve student learning.

But what if you're not familiar with or don't feel ready to teach some areas of digital literacy? Instead of trying to add something else to an already full curriculum, you can start by learning additional digital literacy skills yourself to model in the classroom. After all, if you're not up-to-date with digital literacy, then you cannot teach it to your students. That said, we all have many responsibilities and finding time for formal training when teaching full-time can be challenging. The solution to this dilemma is the same as for your classroom: Find simple ways to incorporate learning about digital literacy into your everyday life. For example, learning additional digital literacy skills can mean participating in professional development, reading education magazines or blogs, talking to your colleagues about digital literacy skills, or simply paying attention to information from technology vendors. While each of these ideas is purposeful, the point we want to keep emphasizing is that they are not meant to take large amounts of your time. Instead, you can pick one or two things you are already doing and swap them out for a digital literacy activity.

As you remember from Chapter 1, ISTE (**getdigitalskills.org**) identifies the key skills digitally literate individuals need as the abilities to:

- Locate information
- Evaluate sources
- Interpret information
- Express ideas
- Communicate with others
- Navigate technology ecosystems

With these key areas in mind, let's consider what starting with ourselves could look like in each of the areas of digital literacy.

Locate Information

Staying up-to-date on technology is hard. The older we all get, the more out of touch we often realize we are. In addition, there are new technologies (like artificial intelligence or augmented reality) and new technology concerns (like awareness of the data economy) about which we need to learn. One simple strategy for staying up to date is to develop a curated professional learning network in the social media platform of your choice. There are many experts who share new information and strategies that they are using. For example, we like to follow #digitalliteracy,

#digitallearners, and #digitalinclusion to see the newest discussion on these topics, as well as resources shared by others. Also, if you have friends who use social media in their work, ask them to meet for coffee, chat about life, and then ask questions about how they use social media, tips they have learned, and new trends they are seeing on the horizon. Attending a conference like the annual ISTELive edtech conference is a great way to learn about new technology from others who are using it for teaching and learning. Podcasts like *Learning Unleashed* and the *EdSurge Podcast* also discuss new research and ideas related to teaching with technology. Likewise, you could follow publications such as *EdSurge* (**edsurge.com**), a digital news and research magazine that often discusses technology.

Many academics also use alert services to stay current and locate new information. For example, Google Scholar (**scholar.google.com**) offers an email alert feature that allows you to sign up for notifications about news on specified topics. Simply do a search in Google Scholar for a topic of interest (like *teaching digital literacy*), and then click the Create Alert option in the Google Scholar navigation. You will then recieve notifications of newly published papers that match this criteria.

Evaluate Sources

Students are taught to evaluate sources, so mastering your ability to evaluate sources is a great first step. Read widely. Pay attention to various sources, and look for the same information to be reported in multiple news outlets. Learn strategies used by fact checkers, such as *lateral reading*. A version of this strategy called the *SIFT Method* (originally called 4 Moves and a Habit) was originally developed by Mike Caulfield (2017) to teach students to develop the habits needed to evaluate information. These habits include checking for previous work on the claim, finding the original source to verify the information, seeing what other people say about the event or topic, tracing any claims or quotes in the story, then circling back to reread again. This strategy takes some practice, but once you can do it with the media you consume, you will be able to teach it to students.

Professional journals are often peer reviewed, meaning their articles and quality of research are evaluated and vetted by experts in the subject's field prior to publication. Although access to many of these sources is restricted to subscription-based databases (often provided by academic libraries at universities), you can also use open-access journals as a strategy for staying current on new research in the field.

Open access is a publishing model that makes scholarly work available at no cost to the readers or institutions, like libraries, that purchase databases of scholarly work. (You can read more about this in Peter Suber's book, *Open Access*.) Many open-access journals comply with peer review processes as well, such as these that often publish work on digital literacy:

- *Computers and Education Open*
- *Educational Technology and Society*
- *The International Journal of Digital Literacy and Digital Compentence (IJDLDC)*
- *Journal of Media Literacy Education*
- *Nordic Journal of Digital Literacy*

Interpret Information

The volume of information available today is staggering: In his book, *Smarter Than You Think*, Thompson (2014) estimated that 3.6 trillion words are composed *every day*. Essentially, we are exposed to too much information with not enough time (or brain power) to process it all. Cazaly (2021) suggested using technology to store what you don't need right away as a strategy to reduce brain clutter. To create your own knowledge system, make use of your information tools, such as the notes app and folders on your phone. To help you start evaluating reporting prespectives when reading the news, purposefully read articles from various sources. Reuters, AP News, BBC, *The Wall Street Journal*, and Bloomberg all have apps that you can save in one folder to make it easy to check them all.

The artificial intelligence (AI) tool ChatGPT is a sophisticated chatbot that can be very helpful when used correctly and with awareness. You can, for example, ask ChatGPT to interpret information for you, such as to summarize data related to the homework gap or to compare coverage of the 2005 Hurricane Katrina disaster from various news channels. The free version of ChatGPT (**chat.openai.com**) does have limitations. Because it cannot browse the internet like a search engine, it cannot interpret the most current information. It can, on the other hand, analyze the sentiment of news, social media posts, or online reviews to identify if the content is positive, negative, or neutral. To generate summaries of articles and videos, you can try YouTube & Article Summary powered by ChatGPT, which is a free Chrome Extension available from Google.

Express Ideas

Pick a new social media site you are curious about, submit an article to a newspaper or magazine, create a newsletter, develop an infographic, or develop digital art. Just try something new that interests you. Many educators share their new ideas and creations on social media sites, like Facebook groups, Threads, Twitter, or Hive. These experiences will help you get feedback from other educators, give you new ideas for instruction, and perhaps give other educators new ideas too.

CONNECTIONS: ISTE STANDARDS

2.4 Collaborator. Educators dedicate time to collaborate with both colleagues and students to improve practice, discover and share resources and ideas, and solve problems.

We try to model this ourselves and have written blog posts and stories to share practices that we are doing. For example, we wrote about a project on digital citizenship we developed and published it in a magazine for other educators (Hays & Kammer, 2023). There are many places to share the important work done in schools that have lasting impact, including blogs or media within your content area. We also invited many teachers to share what they are doing in this book, which you will see as you keep reading!

Communicate with Others

When working with colleagues on a project, propose using a new collaboration tool or use a new feature within collaboration software you already have experience with. Discover new ways to communicate with others without making big changes. Collaboration software includes Google Docs, Microsoft Word in OneDrive, Notion (**notion.so**), Padlet (**padlet.com**), and NowComment (**nowcomment.com**). For example, at a professional development day or if several colleagues are attending a conference, you could create a shared document with Google Docs for all to take notes together. Collaborative note-taking is a strategy used in higher education for documenting classes and events (Patson, 2021). Of course, there are many other tools you may be using and want to explore.

Navigate Technology Ecosystems

Think about the technology that you use at school. How many systems interact with each other? If you were to map this out, what would it look like? For example, when you log in to Schoology (or your learning management system), an authentication system must allow you access. When you send an email through Schoology, it goes to the student's email, which is likely also a school-supported platform, perhaps Microsoft Outlook or Gmail. Your school might also have placed internet filters or security systems on your computer.

Take time to learn about the technology ecosystems of your school and how things work together. Members of the IT staff could provide training, explaining how systems work together and then answering questions. To help keep the training focused, teachers may want to submit questions beforehand as well.

Many digital resources provide built-in navigation tools, like breadcrumbs, taxonomy or controlled vocabulary, or indicators that tell you when the page is loading or how much you have read. Ebooks also offer many features like bookmarking, note-taking, dictionaries, narrating, translating or downloading chapters. Next time you are using one of these tools for reading, take some time to examine these features so that you can point them out to students later when they are using them.

In your personal life, reflect on your use of social media. Go back and read old social media posts. Use the Internet Archive's Wayback Machine (**web.archive.org**) to see what is still available online. Google yourself. These things can help you realize what *digital footprint* (also known as a *digital tattoo*) you have left and can give insight into what actions you want to take in the future. Moorefield-Lang and Lang (2020) described this as *one's digital legacy*. One person may have more than ten accounts on social media. Some may be active, and some dormant. Moorefield-Lang and Craddock (2023) call these *zombie accounts* and recommend cleaning them out like you would clean out a closet.

Emphasize Digital Literacy Where It Is Already Being Used

Most likely, you often use digital literacy without realizing it. By taking notice of what you are doing you can name it for students so that they become more aware of digital literacy skills and mental habits. Consider what this may look like in practice.

You teach first grade. Each day, you get online to take attendance. To do this, you navigate to a specific program on your computer and log in. Today, your login fails. You likely try again, because your first thought is that you typed in your credentials incorrectly. The second time you type your information it works! When you are engaged in this activity, you can briefly share with the students what happened and why you decided to try your credentials again. Through this you can have a brief discussion about case-sensitive logins. This would not take more than a minute or two, and it brings digital literacy habits of mind into the open.

Suppose your credentials still do not work the second time. Now you must start thinking about what else the cause could be. It is not likely you typed your credentials incorrectly twice. So, you pause and think about how often you are required to update your password. Your district has a policy that passwords must be changed every six months. Then you remember that you had to change your password before you left school for the day yesterday, and you need to use your new password. This is an opportunity to explain to students what you were thinking about while you paused. Students need to understand the importance of problem solving and the ability to think through different scenarios when technology problems arise. This is also an opportunity to explain to students why passwords need to be strong and why the district requires you to update your password every six months.

Teachers also frequently ask students to use digital literacy skills without calling them that or explaining why they are asking students to use certain skills. For example, you may ask your students to keep their password secure, use a different software program than you asked them to use last week, or find a news article online. These are just examples, but they demonstrate the simple things asked of students each day that are, in fact, digital literacy. To connect the learning more clearly to digital literacy, you just need to explain why you're asking. Consider what this could look like.

You teach ninth grade. Previously, you had students use Canva (**canva.com**) to create an infographic about a topic they were studying. Today, you want students to create a flier, but instead of pointing them to Canva, you ask them to use Adobe Express (**adobe.com/express**). Students audibly grumble. They liked Canva and do not want to learn a new program. This is a good opportunity to pause the class for a couple minutes and explain that you want them to have many different experiences with technology. While there are many similarities between software programs, there are also differences. You explain that the more they see both the similarities and differences, the easier it will be for them to navigate between platforms and to adjust to new versions. You continue by explaining that graphic design software, just like other types of software categories, have mostly the same user goals, but each has slightly different features that are important to understand. Being able to evaluate software for similarities and differences will make them more productive users of digital technology.

Identify Areas of Low Digital Competence

Another way to integrate digital literacy is to identify areas of low digital competence and move toward improvements. To do this, you will need to begin where both you and your students have low digital competence.

CONNECTIONS: ISTE STANDARDS

2.1 Learner. Educators continually improve their practice by learning from and with others and exploring proven and promising practices that leverage technology to improve student learning.

For yourself, you may not have to think too hard about this. You may know exactly where you do not feel confident with digital literacy. Others of you may feel very confident with digital literacy and need to spend time reflecting on where you can improve. This can also be a good opportunity to talk to colleagues, your professional learning network, or your mentor teacher about what areas they could suggest for you to seek growth opportunities.

Once you have identified at least one area where you want to improve, find ways to enhance your skills. You could watch videos, read articles, talk to colleagues, or just try something new. Be willing to try and to struggle with technology. That is a good mental habit, and it will also help the learning to stick.

As you learn a new skill, share what you are learning with your students. Let them know how important it is to engage in lifelong learning. Some of your students may know more about a particular digital literacy topic than you do, and that is okay! Let them share. Not all of your students will know the same things, so giving digitally savvy students the opportunity to share will build their confidence and help others learn.

For your students, you also need to identify their low areas of digital competence. To start, we suggest thinking broadly. What are areas of digital literacy that much of your class struggles with? One example could be that your class struggles with locating information. They consistently ask for your advice on where to go online. A simple strategy to address this would be to create a list of sources, with explanations of why they are good sources, for students to refer to. Then, when you ask students to engage in a research project, before letting them begin, ask them which sources from the list they believe they will start with and ask them to briefly explain why.

A second way of approaching this is to identify areas of low digital competence among students, then create groups with similar-skilled students and groups with varied-skilled students. In other words, provide differentiated instruction related to digital literacy.

For similar-skilled groups, give them additional guidance or boundaries for their work. Suppose the assignment is for students to create information in a visual manner. One group of students struggles with expressing ideas in a digital format, so you provide them with an infographic template to organize their thoughts. Another group is more advanced with expressing ideas in a digital format, so you ask them to use a blank Google Slides presentation.

For varied-skilled groups, you can use a jigsaw lesson to support student growth with digital literacy. As you assign groups, take the digital literacy skills of the students into consideration and group two students with lower digital literacy skills with two students who have higher digital literacy skills. Additionally, as you assign topics within each group, make sure that students with lower digital literacy are partnered with students with higher digital literacy skills in the expert groups. Therefore, students are always working with a varied-skilled group. As groups research their topics, ask them to pause at various times and explain how they are searching for information, how they are evaluating it, and how they are interpreting information with others in their group. With this approach, students can share strategies, and everyone can hear about digital literacy without taking the focus off the content being learned.

Ask Students to Use Digital Literacy and Teach It

This is where the explicit instruction of digital literacy comes into play. On a day-to-day basis many activities in the classroom require digital literacy. As you think about where you may want and need to incorporate direct digital literacy instruction, we encourage you to start at the beginning—the beginning of the school year.

If your school is 1:1, spend time going over how to log in, access apps, and use various software platforms you will have students engage with throughout the year. Plan at least five minutes for practice each time you start using an app for the first couple of weeks. Then gradually, you can back off and expect students to know what to do.

Take time at the beginning of the school year to show students how to access their email, the learning management system, and any other program you expect students to be able to use. Consider giving a short quiz over how to access tools, or have students create a screen recording (assuming they know how to do this) demonstrating their knowledge of the software they need to know. These are opportunities to reinforce learning, and the actions of retrieval practice (see Chapter 2) students use to complete the quiz or screen recording will help move the digital literacy skills into long-term memory.

Additionally, consider setting aside time at the beginning of the school year to establish norms around the use of technology. For example, discuss the appropriate use of technology and your expectations for how students behave online and how they handle physical equipment. This could be everything from coming to class with their tablet charged to treating others the way they want to be treated. Developing a user policy that students sign at the beginning of the year can be a positive way of setting these norms.

> **CONNECTIONS**
> ## Partnering with Librarians
>
> Partnering with your school librarians/media specialist is another way of integrating digital literacy instruction directly into teaching. School librarians are experts at locating information, evaluating sources, and navigating technology ecosystems. Use that expertise! You can partner with your school librarian in the following ways:
>
> - **Assignment design:** Librarians can help you design a lesson for locating sources.
> - **Showcasing student digital literacy skills:** Ask librarians if they have time to create a digital (e.g., website or social media account) or physical (e.g., bulletin board) space to showcase the digital literacy skills your students are learning and using. These can be great opportunities to encourage digital literacy in the school.
> - **Guest speaker:** Ask your school librarian to share their knowledge of locating information, evaluating sources, and navigating technology ecosystems with your students.
> - **Help you stay up to date:** Even if your school librarian does not help directly with digital literacy instruction, they can be an excellent resource for sharing content and helping you stay current.

Opportunities: Old and New

Every year new students walk into your classroom with their own backgrounds and experiences. You must learn about your students to meet them where they are and help them achieve the learning goals for the year. This means that growing digital literacy in your students may feel like you are starting over every year, and just like with every other topic you teach, you are. However, you are not starting over with yourself. Each year, you will become more comfortable integrating digital literacy into your teaching. You will learn more simple strategies to quickly draw upon and use. Let's consider what these can look like for old opportunities and new opportunities.

MEMES
A Simple Strategy

Teacher- or student-created memes teach students to communicate digitally, express ideas, and use functional digital literacy skills involving creating digital artifacts. Memes, a multimodal form of digital writing, are used in classrooms to build connections between students and learning content, often using humor (one of the habits of mind discussed in Chapter 1). When students create memes, they are able to demonstrate their understanding between text and images, as well as express themselves culturally. In an L2 setting (students learning a second language), students can also demonstrate their understanding of language using memes as a communication medium (Ryu et al., 2022).

In addition, students encounter memes in the real world, some multiple times a day as they use social media. Having awareness about this type of messaging, can prepare students for critically evaluating this type of information in the real world, sometimes referred to as *meme literacy*. Students can learn to pause and reflect on the accuracy of statements made in the meme or if the meme is being used with specific intentions. As Figure 3.1 illustrates, many quotes in memes are false quotes, misattributed quotes, or misquotes (Carillo, 2019).

FIGURE 3.1
Memes can be an opportunity for students to demonstrate learning, or critically reflect on accuracy of information, as pictured in this meme (Abraham Lincoln Gives Life Lessons, 2021).

What Is SAMR?

SAMR is a teaching model created by Ruben Puentedura (2006) to help teachers to think about how technology supports learning in their classrooms. SAMR stands for: Substitution, Augmentation, Modification, and Redefinition. The tiered model encourages teachers to recognize the level in which they are using technology and to switch to using technology with more sophistication and in more transformative ways (Figure 3.2). For example, teachers can simply replace their print materials with digital materials (Substitution level) or they can redefine lessons with technology by creating new and transformative teaching strategies, like adding a virtual field trip to the Louvre during a lesson on the Renaissance (Redefinition level).

SAMR is a helpful model for integrating digital literacy (though not as simple!). When teachers increase their use of technology to use it in more sophisticated ways, the student is able to use more digital literacy skills and grow digital competence.

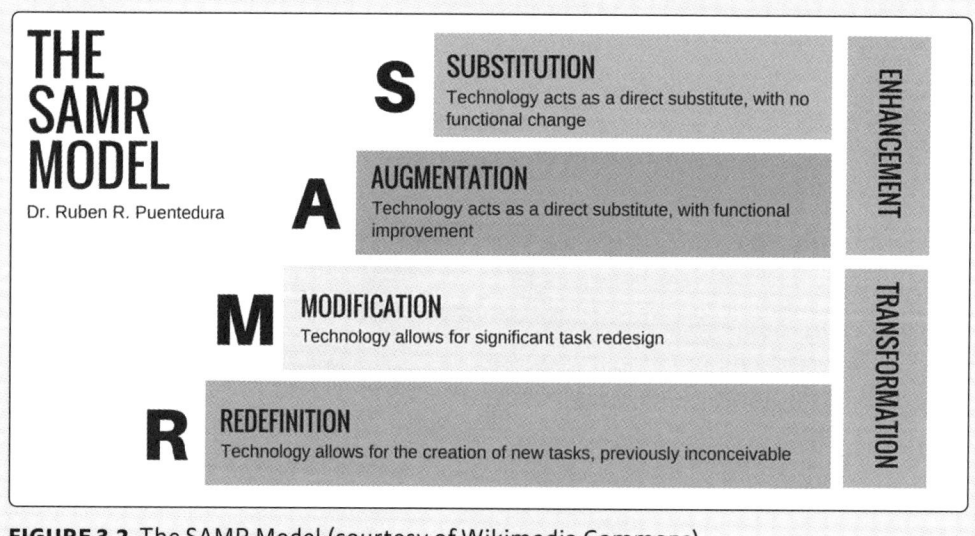

FIGURE 3.2 The SAMR Model (courtesy of Wikimedia Commons)

Old Opportunities

There are many opportunities for integrating digital literacy into your classroom that already exist. This means finding opportunities to enhance existing lessons with digital literacy. Each class is going to look different. As content experts, teachers can examine the subject areas they teach for digital literacy opportunities (see Chapter 4 for more examples of this). For now, here are some simple strategies to consider that fit within all learning contexts:

- Rework activities to allow students to include their own digital research.
- Name digital literacy skills as you have students use them. For example, if students are using multiple sources with different perspectives to understand a topic, explain that they are using the digital literacy skill of interpreting information.
- Describe digital literacy habits of mind as you use them. For example, if using a meme in class, ask students to evaluate why you may have used that meme (and ask them how well that worked for them!). In addition, a meme is a combination of words and images to convey a message. What is that message? Does the message change if the image changes? By encouraging some reflection, you can help students develop mental habits to think about the work they are consuming or creating.
- Use a technology framework to integrate digital literacy (e.g., SAMR [Puentedura, 2006], the Technology Integration Matrix [Florida Center for Instructional Technology, 2019]).

New Opportunities

To identify digital literacy gaps for your students, examine your own experiences. This simple strategy of identifying gaps and finding solutions is how many digital instructional resources have been developed. For example, high school Latin teacher Ben Johnson noticed that the his students' skill at scanning the metric structure of ancient poetry improved with practice and instant feedback. To provide students with both practice and feedback, he created the Hexameter website (**hexameter.co**) and filled it with poetry to scan. Instead of playing Wordle or Chess during down time, students play this game, which increases their Latin content knowledge—and increases their digital literacy at the same time. Leveraging its rating system (scanning a line correctly raises a student's rating), the site is able to deliver customized practice at each user's level. As students gain ability, they also get more difficult lines to practice as well as badges, which are rewards for milestones and success. And while the site can be used entirely separate from the classroom, there are tools set up to allow for discussion by a class and for students to save lines for later review with their teacher. This teacher identified an area of low competence and addressed it with a new opportunity, which is improving Latin skills *and* digital literacy!

Now, other Latin teachers can use this resource as one of their simple strategies: They can assign this digital resource and encourage students to critically describe what they are learning and how they are improving while using it. In Table 3.1, you can see how integrating Hexameter.co into instruction can develop digital literacy as it expands into the Four Corners Framework (Designer 2.5.a).

TABLE 3.1 Aligning Hexameter.co with the Four Corners Framework

INTEGRATION	A high school Latin teacher assigns Hexameter.co to his students for practice while teaching scansion (the process of reading Latin poetry using sound and metrics).
CULTURE	Because Hexameter.co is available outside of the school, other students in Latin classes in other schools and states may have experience with it. The students have this in common when they meet other Latin students at Junior Classical League (JCL) conventions. College Latin teachers can expect that students who had Latin in high school have used the game.
MODELING	The teacher introduces Hexameter.co by modeling from the teacher account, then allows students to practice on their individual accounts. The teacher will float around the classroom to help students with skills, sometimes clarifying before a student submits, sometimes explaining what happened if they get it wrong.
MENTORSHIP	Students enjoy the game-like features of Hexameter.co and work on it when they need in a break. Students are able to explain the concepts to each other and help their classmates while using it.

There are also opportunities for integrating digital literacy in your classroom that can be added over time. This means either reworking existing lessons or developing new lessons for digital literacy integration. Just as with old opportunities, new opportunities are going to look different in every learning context. Here are some simple strategies to consider for new opportunities that fit within all learning contexts:

- Add bell work that asks students to use digital literacy skills such as having students search a news site for a current event to share or create digital artwork related to something discussed in class using DALL·E 2 (an AI tool that can create realistic images; **openai.com/dall-e-2**). Students can prompt DALL·E 2 to create a solution to a problem (like a graphic of a futuristic building with a food forest as a solution to hunger) or a visual representation of classroom topic (like a 3D render of walking on the moon after learning about space).

- Ask students to journal about the digital literacy habits of mind they use when completing an assignment. They can keep their journal in a digital tool, such as Blogger (**blogger.com**) or use a pencil and paper. The key is to make sure students are reflecting on the mental habits they use when using technology, such as persisting when challenged, having a growth mindset, taking breaks when needed, seeking rewards, having fun, communicating, or sharing.

- Have students teach a peer about a digital literacy skill. For example, one student may be good at creating tables in Microsoft Word or Google Docs. Ask them to share that knowledge with a student who is unsure how to create a table.

  Work with teachers across grade levels to understand what digital literacy skills and mental habits the students in your class have already learned (see Table 3.2).

- Work as a grade-level team or subject-matter team to determine what digital literacy skills and mental habits you will integrate.

TABLE 3.2 Where Digital Literacy Skills Intersect with Habits of Mind

Habits of Mind	Locate Information	Evaluate Sources	Interpret Information	Express Ideas	Communicate with Others	Navigate Technology Ecosystems
Thinking about your thinking (metacognition)	x	x	x	x		x
Persisting	x	x	x	x	x	x
Managing impulsivity		x	x	x		x
Striving for accuracy	x	x	x	x	x	x
Listening with understanding and empathy					x	
Thinking flexibly	x	x	x	x	x	x
Questioning and posing problems		x		x		
Thinking interdependently	x	x	x	x	x	x
Thinking and communicating with clarity and precision				x	x	
Applying past knowledge to new situations	x	x	x	x	x	x
Gathering data through all senses		x	x			
Creating, imaging, and innovating				x	x	
Taking responsible risks				x	x	x
Responding with wonderment and awe			x	x	x	
Remaining open to continuous learning	x	x	x	x	x	x

There are many pedagogical activities that teachers already do that align to the habits of mind (see Table 3.3). While this table focuses on specific activities, you can think about pedagogy more broadly and consider what educational philosophies promote as well. For example, social learning theory may promote curiosity, behaviorism may promote striving for accuracy, so we encourage you to take a step back and think about the philosophies underlying your teaching and what mental habits it may be promoting.

TABLE 3.3 Alignment of Activities and the Habits of Mind

PEDAGOGICAL ACTIVITY	HABIT OF MIND
Journals	Metacognition (thinking about thinking)
Group work	Thinking interdependently
Storytelling	Finding humor
Blogs, social media	Lifelong learning
Presentations	Clear communication
Case studies	Problem solving

Build Community with Digital Experiences

Digital literacy skills can be built through the creation of community in your class. Modeling and mentoring, which are discussed in detail Chapters 5 and 6, play a large role in this, and you can also integrate digital literacy into practices you already do to develop community.

At the beginning of class, for example, you may take time to learn about your students. Many students enjoy sharing about themselves, but others are shy and not comfortable revealing information. To address these differences, consider including both a face-to-face sharing and a virtual project. For example, in an elementary class, you could do an About Me sheet that students fill out and share with the class. Then you can also have students create a piece of digital art that they feel represents them. This gives you the opportunity to build community and teach students about tools to create digital art.

Early in the class, we think it is a good idea to collect information about the digital literacy skills your students already possess. Many of you may already have students complete a survey so that you can learn more about them. You might ask their interests, preferred name, favorite subject in school, and so on. We suggest adding a few questions about digital literacy, such as:

- Where do you search for information online?
- What websites do you frequently visit?
- What is the technology skill you are most proud of?
- What technology skill do you want to learn?
- What tools have you used to complete your homework?
- What social media sites do you use? Which is your favorite?
- How do you stay safe online?

This information can be useful for you as you think about integrating digital literacy skills. Additionally, this information can be beneficial as you create groups or assign partners for activities. Depending on your goals for an activity, you may want to partner students together with similar skills or dissimilar skills so that they can learn from each other.

You may also want to use this data for grouping students at tables. When creating a seating plan, you may want to think about students who have similar digital interests, or you may want to put people together with varying digital interests and encourage them to share and demonstrate the tools they use to complete homework or sites they visit to search for information. This can be done as bell work.

Examples of Integrated Digital Literacy

As you remember from Chapter 1, ISTE identifies the key skills digitally literate individuals need as the abilities to locate information, evaluate sources, interpret information, express ideas, communicate with others and navigate technology ecosystems (**getdigitalskills.org**). The sections that follow offer simple examples of integrating these digital literacy skills.

Example 1: Communicate with Others

Jasmine is teaching a unit on rocks. She has a lesson scheduled with a geologist using Skype a Scientist (**skypeascientist.com**). Before the lesson, she leads a short discussion about digital communication technologies and how they allow people to connect with others all over the world. She asks students to think about how they should behave when using digital communication technologies, and they brainstorm ideas. The class suggests the following behavior: Take turns speaking, introduce yourself, confirm the other person can hear you, and say goodbye before hanging up.

Example 2: Navigate Technology Ecosystems

All year, Derek has been using Padlet (**padlet.com**) for students to post questions they have about books they are reading as a class. Essentially a virtual bulletin board for sharing content and comments, the tool has been working very well, and students are actively engaged. Now that it is April, Derek thinks he may want to introduce a different tool so that students gain familiarity with another similar tool. He wants students to be able to comfortably move to different user interfaces while staying focused on content. Because students are doing such a good job thinking about the books and asking questions, he decides now is the time to try a different tool. He creates a jam (a digital whiteboard) with Google Jamboard (**jamboard.google.com**) and asks students to post their questions to it. Before giving students access to the jam, he briefly shows where in Jamboard they can find tools similar to those they use in Padlet and makes connections between functionalities.

Example 3: Express Ideas

Jessica teaches ELA, and her students frequently write papers. Most students write their papers using Google Docs, but she knows they also will need familiarity with Microsoft Word as they move into the workforce. She is not sure that all her students have access to Word, so she schedules time in the library computer lab. In the lab, she shows students key features of Word, and then asks them to use it to write a brief reflection on a YouTube video she showed. Throughout the year, Jessica schedules days in the lab and asks students to write using Word.

CONNECTIONS

Emerging Technology for Digital Experiences

The trouble with emerging technologies is they're always changing as the once new becomes commonplace and a new "new" takes its place. How do you keep up? Start with investigating topics yourself, then share with your students. The emerging may already be used more widely than you or they think. Here are a few currently emerging technologies to think about integrating or discussing in your classroom.

- **Virtual Reality (VR):** The phrase *virtual reality* probably calls to mind a fully immersive experience that takes place when someone is wearing a headset. While this high-end implementation of the technology can be found in some classrooms, it is not the only way to introduce students to VR. A simple strategy for moving toward virtual reality is using 360-degree videos. These videos allow a viewer to pan around and see a recorded space from multiple perspectives, as if standing at the bottom of the Grand Canyon and looking around, for example. While not immersive, these videos do give students the opportunity to see more of a space and interact with it. You can find 360-degree videos on YouTube and produced by National Geographic, BBC, NASA, and Discovery among others.

- **Artificial Intelligence (AI):** You are likely using artificial intelligence already and may not realize it. For instance, predictive text (i.e., suggested text when writing an email or on a document) is one example of AI. Personalized learning in online curriculum is another. Instead of diving into a big new way to add AI to your classroom, such as learning ChatGPT or DALL·E 2, take time to point out small examples of artificial intelligence and machine learning that are already there.

- **Metaverse:** A 3D virtual space for playing, socializing, and learning, the metaverse is likely years away or may never materialize as it has been written about in fiction or shown in movies. However, smaller examples are with us today in the form of the shared, immersive gaming worlds of Minecraft and Fortnight. Plus, we think we can all agree that the future will bring more options and innovations for virtual meetings and meeting spaces than currently exist. A simple strategy for helping students understand the metaverse and what *might* be coming is to have students read fictional accounts of life in a metaverse (e.g., *Ready Player One*). Giving students a vision of what the future could look like will help give them context and help them develop ideas.

The Research

Research on evaluating information has expanded as discussions around the concerns related to misinformation have increased.

- **Research on evaluating information.** The Stanford group found that using tools such as the CRAAP (Currency, Relevance, Authority, Accuracy, and Purpose) Test are ineffective at teaching students how to evaluate sources. The CRAAP Test asked students to look at the entirety of a webpage to evaluate it. However, that strategy does not work when content can be changed or made to look the way the authors desire. Instead, sources need to be evaluated against the content from other sites. The SIFT method—Stop, Investigate the source, Find better coverage, and Trace claims, quotes, and media back to the original context—is a tool for teaching students to develop their lateral reading skills to better evaluate sources. The Check, Please! Starter Course website is a SIFT tutorial that was developed to teach students how to fact and source-check media (scan the QR code to learn more).

SIFT TUTORIAL

- **A call for ideas.** The Rita Allen Foundation held a Misinformation Solutions Forum in 2018 which invited creative interventions to reduce the influence of such misinformation as false advertising, fabricated news stories or social media posts, and deep fakes. Six finalists and three winning teams were selected to develop digital literacy projects to reduce the spread of misinformation. Many of these ideas were developed and are available for educators to use with their students. Scan the QR code to learn more.

MISINFORMATION SOLUTIONS FORUM

- **Research on evaluating information.** Lateral reading is another strategy you can use to teach students about evaluating information. Used in journalism for fact checking, *lateral reading* is the practice of reading across websites instead of staying on only one site. A person opens many tabs to check different sources and content to determine if they all say similar things about a topic. Scan the QR code to learn more about lateral reading and evaluating online sources.

LATERAL VS. VERTICAL READING

Chapter 3 Takeaways

In this section, the important takeaways from the chapter are paired with the ISTE Standards for Educators that inform them.

- It is important to build your own digital literacy skills and knowledge before you can integrate digital literacy in your classroom (Learner 2.1.a, 2.1.c).
- Digital literacy can be incorporated into existing lessons and regular activities throughout the day (Designer 2.5.a).
- You may already be using technology in your classroom. A little more focus on the digital literacy elements of these activities can increase the opportunities for students to learn digital literacy (Citizen 2.3.a).

Reflection

Before moving on, take some time to consider how the ideas in Chapter 3 apply within your context using the questions below.

- What digital literacy skill or habit of mind do you want to start with yourself?
- Where could you learn more about it?
- Where is digital literacy already being used in your classroom? Where do you want to emphasize it?
- Where do students have low digital competence?
- In what ways do you want to explicitly teach digital literacy? How will you ask students to use the digital literacy skills or habits of mind you are teaching them?

CHAPTER 4

Developing a Culture of Digital Literacy

KEY ISTE STANDARDS

This chapter addresses these ISTE Standards for Educators:

- Leader 2.2.a
- Collaborator 2.5.a

By the end of this chapter, you will:

- Understand the challenges of teaching digital literacy and how working together can help to solve them.
- Understand the opportunities for educators in various roles to support digital literacy across the school.
- Start to view yourself as a critical component of the digital literacy ecosystem.
- Understand the theory- and research-based rationale for working within a culture of digital literacy.

Digital Literacy Is Contextual

It could be argued that all modern schools now have a digital culture. Teachers use many technologies every day to do their jobs. On a typical day, you probably set up the technology for your first class before students even arrive. You may need to log time in a human resources application, upload worksheets to a learning management system, communicate with parents on ClassDojo (**ClassDojo.com**), create a presentation for the digital whiteboard, assign readings from a digital curricular resource and take attendance in attendance tracking software.

Students also use many technologies every day in school. For example, a student may start the day using their own mobile device to communicate with friends or catch up on YouTube videos. Then at school, they may log in to their school-issued device to play a game in Gimkit (**gimkit.com**), check the learning management system for due dates, or check their grades in the student information system.

One criticism of the term *digital literacy* is that it implies that one is either literate or illiterate with digital skills. In fact, digital literacy is contextual. One may have high digital literacy in spreadsheets but have low digital literacy in using a VR headset. A teacher may be excellent at creating digital instructional materials but uncomfortable running a Kahoot! (**kahoot.com**) presentation in class. In this chapter, we unpack how a learning culture can help to ensure that digital literacy becomes more of a growth mindset, rather than a label, which can improve as the school community utilizes the strengths of others.

Challenges to Teaching Digital Literacy

The sudden shift to remote, technology-based teaching at the start of the COVID-19 pandemic illuminated the challenges of teaching digital literacy in schools. Teachers who were used to face-to-face classes suddenly had to teach online, which requires a completely different set of teaching skills and tools. In addition, young students had to pivot to learning in their own homes, an environment typically reserved for leisure and family time. Teachers had to relearn how to deliver their content, while students had to reimagine their home life to include schooling, which included curating resources to learn online, finding learning spaces at home to work, and learning how to learn online. If a school was not already technologically equipped with devices, a strong broadband system, and digitally competent teachers, then the pivot to remote learning was more challenging. Even for schools that were well prepared, families still struggled with using some of the educational systems.

The Digital Divide

The term *digital divide* is used to describe unequal access to technology. Each student's home may have varying access to smartphones, laptops, desktops, digital resources, and the internet. van Dijk & Hacker (2003) suggested that moving toward standards-based learning increased the digital divide as some geographic areas had greater access to the internet, funding to purchase and provide technology, and access to community resources with technology. In theory, providing technology to the people should create equity and reduce technical and economic barriers. Research has since found, however, that access alone is not enough to close the digital divide and that educators and information professionals (teachers and librarians) must work to help individuals learn how to use technology for information, communication, and creating new knowledge (Aqili & Moghaddam, 2008). For example, Boser (2013) reported that while low-income, non-white children used technology for basic drills and practice exercises, more affluent youth were able to use technology in more meaningful ways such as problem-solving and higher-order thinking.

In the book *Closing the Gap: Digital Equity Strategies for the K–12 Classroom*, it was explained that even as technology gaps close, there is still the digital-use gap (Thomas, et al., 2018). Some students have more access to digital mentors (and from an earlier age) than others, and those students tend to use technology for more meaningful learning than those who don't. Hiefield and Carter (2021) recommend that teachers avoid using technology for "drill and kill" to prepare students for tests and instead use technology to build research and inquiry skills, which will encourage less boredom, support critical thinking, and prepare them for lifelong learning outside of the classroom.

The research related to the challenges of teaching digital literacy has long established that the school infrastructure and teacher digital competence are two of the biggest challenges for digital initiatives in schools. If we think back to the influences in Figure 2.1, each of these challenges can have an impact on the digital literacy attained by students. For example, if the infrastructure does not support digital literacy, then students are unable to grow while they are in that environment.

Even though digital competence is essential for teaching, teachers tend to self-report low levels of digital competence. Sánchez-Cruzado et al. (2021) found that when they asked teachers to self-report their own digital competency during remote learning, many of the teachers reported very low digital competence. Using the DigComp 2.0 Framework, a European Digital Competence Framework designed to improve citizen's digital competence, they explained that teacher digital competence can be organized into five fields (Sánchez-Cruzado et al., 2021, p. 4):

- **Information and Information Literacy:** Identify, locate, retrieve, store, organize and analyze digital information, assessing its relevance and purpose for teaching needs.
- **Communication and Collaboration:** Communicate in digital environments, share resources via online tools, connect and collaborate with others through digital tools, and interact and participate in communities and networks, promoting intercultural awareness.
- **Creation of Digital Content:** Create and edit new digital content; integrate and rebuild prior knowledge and content; make artistic productions, multimedia content, and computer programming; and apply intellectual property rights and licenses.
- **Security:** Protect personal information and data, protect digital identity and digital content, understand security measures, and exercise responsible and safe use of technology.
- **Problem Resolution:** Identify needs in the use of digital resources, make informed decisions about the most appropriate digital tool depending on the purpose or need, solve conceptual problems through digital media or digital tools, and use technology.

Collaborating Across the School for Digital Literacy

The good news is that many schools have staff who are experts in the various areas of digital competence. By working together and understanding how educators in other roles are trained in specific areas, a digital learning culture can emerge. The first part of considering how to maximize the learning culture in a school is to understand the different agents in the schools and their involvement in digital literacy.

Classroom Teacher

Classroom teachers are highly trained in school and professional development on the newest technology and how to use it. They also use technology to communicate with their learning community, which includes parents and students. However, they may have different comfort and interest levels in integrating it into their instruction and differing abilities for using it to create educational content. While some teachers may want to use only a digital lightboard for presenting to students, others prefer to teach with digital games or even integrate design thinking, which can be applied to creating with technology. Classroom teachers often share what they have learned with each other and help each other as needed. In addition, they often have a support person of their choice who they contact within the school for help using technology. Teachers have high digital competence in communication and collaboration.

School Librarian

School librarians are educators who are also trained in information and media literacy, information resources, intellectual freedom, and inquiry. They are also often the technology experts in the school, being adept at using technology for learning as well as skilled at understanding the implications of technology. The school librarian has a mission to support students in the information seeking process, one which requires digital literacy skills.

Technology Coach

Technology coaches are educators who work specifically with teachers, helping them to teach with technology in their classrooms. Technology coaches are trained in collaboration, student-centered approaches, and technology-enabled learning. If a building has a technology coach, that person may be the one primarily supporting teachers' digital literacy in schools, as well as offering guidance for integrating digital literacy into instruction. Technology coaches are able to model learning and work with technology, as well as encourage the development of digital learning experiences and assessments. School librarians and technology coaches have high digital competence in information literacy and creation of digital content.

Information Technology Staff

Every school has information technology (IT) staff who maintain the technology for the school's digital resources, including the internet connection, security, privacy, accessibility, internet filters, firewalls, storage, and the physical devices used within the school. IT staff often provide technical support to stakeholders and engage in purchasing technology, as well as integrating different systems (such as integrating the school information system with the library catalog). IT staff have high digital competence in security.

Administrator

Administrators include principals, coordinators, directors, and other leadership positions related to leading or supporting technology initiatives. Support from administration is critical to provide the funding, technical support and learning culture to ensure that a digital initiative will work. Administrators often advocate, secure funding, and develop scheduling critical to innovation in schools. Administrators at the school and district level are responsible for ensuring that school staff have adequate professional development for learning to use technology and professional development for teaching digital literacy. In addition, administrators are critical for establishing clear expectations for effective use of technology with students. In this role, administrators should also be aware of the flow of technology and digital skills instruction throughout the school. An administrator must have high digital competence in problem resolution.

Support Staff

Support staff can include secretaries, paraprofessionals, office workers, or any staff members who interact with students, parents, and teachers. At any time, support staff may be asked questions related to technical support or using school technology to use the internet, access grades, view reports, communicate, or submit paperwork. Support staff who interact with the parent community often know the major challenges that parents and students are experiencing at home related to using school issued devices or software. Support staff have a strong understanding of the challenges that users face daily.

CONNECTIONS
Digital Learning Day

Since 2012, Digital Learning Day (#DLDay) has been an annual effort lead by All4Ed and Future Ready Schools where schools showcase their digital learning strategies (**all4ed.org/digital-learning-day**). While a culture of digital literacy is not limited to just one day, Digital Learning Day is one way to showcase the school's efforts related to digital literacy, ultimately leading to increased awareness and innovation within the school. Some of the ways that you can participate in Digital Learning Day are to:

- Showcase a favorite digital tool on Twitter with hashtag #DLDay.
- Attend a professional development session hosted by All4Ed on Digital Learning Day.
- Work with a tech coach or school librarian to set up a sharing board to share technology within the district or school to get new ideas from others, and share your own ideas.
- Involve students by hosting a contest involving technology, like video creation, stop motion animation, or coding.
- Set up a greenscreen for students to celebrate digital learning day by taking their own photos (and editing them).
- Choose one lesson that day and add an element of digital literacy to it. For example, if students are writing poetry, invite the school librarian to show students how to search the library catalog to find books in the school library with poetry in them.

Collaboration Between Educators

Did you know that collaboration is part of all the strands of the Future Ready Framework? It is, because through collaboration we can change a school's culture, including better support of digital literacy. Collaboration makes it possible to do more than can be done alone and provides a sense of community amongst those who do collaborate. In addition, students benefit from increased learning transfer as educators can build upon concepts as students move between classes.

CONNECTIONS: ISTE STANDARDS

2.4 Collaborator. Educators dedicate time to collaborate with both colleagues and students to improve practice, discover and share resources and ideas, and solve problems.

Collaborating for digital literacy is the intentional effort to work together to implement digital literacy in various school settings. Not to be confused with collaboration as a digital literacy skill, collaborating between educators to teach digital literacy has potential to increase impact, while also creating a more seamless integration of digital literacy for students. Collaboration can occur at various levels, such as:

- Networking
- Cooperation
- Coordination
- Full collaboration

Table 4.1, which was adapted from Frey et al. (2006) for digital literacy initiatives, takes a closer look at each level.

TABLE 4.1 Levels of Collaboration

LEVEL	NETWORKING	COOPERATION	COORDINATION	FULL COLLABORATION
Description	Educators talk to each other and share practice.	Educators informally support each other's activities.	Educators work together on mutual projects that benefit all.	Educators create a formal agreement and work toward a shared vision.
How does this look for teaching digital literacy?	Educators share what they are doing to address digital literacy at meetings or other group settings. Educators share tools and strategies that work for them.	Educators share and exchange equipment or materials as others need it. Educators observe each other using technology. Educators promote each other's use of technology.	Educators work together on technology committees. Educators coordinate digital projects to further develop them. Educators use scope and sequence to build on digital skills.	Educators develop outcomes with the intention of distributing them in various classrooms. Educators combine resources to acquire technology or teach digital skills. Educators create training programs to develop digital skills.

What does collaboration look like in action? Look no further than Nina Boyett, a media assistant at Newport High School, who is working to develop a culture of digital literacy in her school (personal communication, March 19, 2023). To do this, she has tried to make the library a comfortable place for students to spend time before and after school, as well as during lunch. This has led to other teachers bringing their classes to the library for free-choice reading; a strategy known to increase student digital literacy is enabling students to search for what they like to read! To continue to build the culture of digital literacy, Boyett has joined the district's Computer Science for All (C/S for All) group, which emphasizes teaching technology as an important issue. The library will serve as a central point for technology support and management as the school increases their technological infrastructure with new equipment and devices. Boyett recognizes that this will be a great opportunity for teaching digital literacy and collaborating with other educators. Table 4.2 includes an example of how these simple strategies might look with the Four Corners Framework.

TABLE 4.2 Alignment with the Four Corners Framework (Designer 2.5.a)

INTEGRATION	An English teacher is able to create free-choice reading time in class, and co-teaches with the school librarian who shows students how to use readers advisory websites (like NoveList; ebsco.com/novelist) and the library catalog to find a book they want to read.
CULTURE	This collaboration between the English teacher and librarian has lead to the librarian creating more reading spaces in the library, as well as spaces for students to charge their laptops and phones, or access the library catalog on a tablet. Students are now using this space and resources in class, but also before and after school.
MODELING	To show the students how to use reader advisory websites to find the next book to read, the librarian models how this might be done with one example of a book in a series. After this demonstration, the librarian then models how to find this book in the library catalog, and retrieve it from the shelf. Students also model independent reading as they enjoy the library space with the book they found.
MENTORSHIP	Mentorship can happen at many levels in this scenario. First, the school librarian is able to mentor the teacher on using library resources, and the teacher is able to mentor the school librarian on student interests. Students are also able to help each other by sharing their favorite reader's advisory sites, and talking about the books they are reading.

Digital Literacy Within the Disciplines

While many digital literacy skills, like evaluating sources or communicating online, are transferable to other disciplines, some skills are more critical for accomplishing deeper learning within each discipline (see Table 4.3). For example, as a history concept, a student may need to understand the *digital footprint* (also referred to as a *digital tattoo*) as a modern strategy for documenting historical information. This could also be used to introduce the concept of primary sources and how historical information was gathered before the internet. Table 4.3 elaborates on other content areas.

TABLE 4.3 Unique Digital Literacy Concerns Within Major Content Areas

CONTENT AREA	Unique Digital Literacy Concerns
READING & LANGUAGE ARTS	As students learn to read, they rely on the technical skills to use ebooks and e-resources, but also the tools built within these resources that enable them to define words, hear pronunciations, annotate, or navigate within the interface. In addition, digital literacy for reading involves being able to use tools to find new items that interest readers and assess if what they are reading is true (Picton et al., 2022).
MATH	In math, students need to pose a question, gather data, analyze it and then enterprise the results. This requires knowledge of e-resources to solve problems appropriately, as well as technical skills for using technology for math (Kim How et al., 2022).
SCIENCE	In science, digital literacy involves technical knowledge of equipment, such as digital microscopes and evaluation of reliable sources, as well as the ability to create such multimodal representations as diagrams, concept maps, tables, graphs, and three-dimensional models (Göjdas & Çam, 2022; Ng, 2011).
SOCIAL STUDIES	Students of social studies use digital literacy to evaluate authenticity and credibility of content and digital resources, which help them to learn the concepts of direction, location, and place to understand their communities and cities. They must also understand primary sources, maps, and media (Manfra & Holmes, 2020).

Digital Literacy Across the Disciplines

We co-edited a book for higher education educators that described how digital literacy is taught in various disciplines and with the intention of preparing students for a career that will likely include technology and digital skills (Hays & Kammer, 2021a). The presumption was that digital literacy is woven throughout all content areas and that the opportunities for teaching digital literacy are abundant in higher education. In K–12 schools, this is even more so as students often visit many different educators within the building on a regular basis.

Hobbs and Coiro (2016) recommend the WOVEN (Written, Oral, Visual, Electronic, and Nonverbal) communication approach, a teaching strategy used at Georgia Tech to emphasize creating ideas in multiple modes. This multimodal approach builds digital and media literacy in students as they learn to communicate and collaborate using a variety of media, including print and digital. In K–12 grades, WOVEN can be used within one classroom or across classrooms. For example, students may learn to write a script for a video in an English class (written communication), deliver that script in a speech class (oral communication), design slides and visuals for the video in an art class (visual communication), add sound and media in a music class (electronic communication), then introduce the video to parents at an event using nonverbal skills. (Scan the QR code for more detail.)

In an article describing how librarians build community, King and Kammer (2023) shared one example of how this interdisciplinary collaboration might look within an elementary school. In this example, a school in St. Charles, MO, has a student-created morning broadcast, which is organized by the school librarian in collaboration with other teachers whose students are creating content. These students learn many of the communication skills that are also part of WOVEN as they implement all modalities of communication when creating the broadcast, made possible by the support of a network of creative educators.

GEORGIA TECH'S WOVEN APPROACH

Critical Considerations for Technology Use

Most of the discussion in this book has been about using technology in schools. However, the modern education system relies on technology use outside of the school building as well. Technology and connectivity, coupled with the digital skills to use it, are increasingly important for educational opportunity. Students need technology at home to do their homework, access coursework on snow days, or even take online courses as they get older. Parents also use technology to access student grades, communicate with teachers, and communicate with the schools. Teachers also rely on technology to do their job away from the building, whether that means teaching remotely or creating content for class.

The problem is that although many low- and moderate-income families do have access to the internet, they may only have access through their mobile devices and may experience inconsistent connectivity. Rideout and Katz (2016) found that this inequity was even more pronounced for immigrant Hispanic families who indicated that they do not get online at all. This report also found that children who had inconsistent access to the internet were also less likely to pursue their own educational interests while at home or use technology to create their own art or music.

During the COVID-19 pandemic, many schools that did not already provide mobile devices for students purchased them with COVID relief funding (U.S. Department of Education, 2021). One survey found that in 2021, 90% of schools had one device for every middle and high schooler, with 84% providing them for elementary students (Klein, 2021). This same survey found that many schools were not planning on heavily using 1:1 devices after remote learning ceased and students were back in the classroom, due to maintenance of devices and alternatives to working on screens.

> **CONNECTIONS**
> ## Distributing Digital Literacy in Schools
>
> The African proverb "It takes a village to raise a child" conveys the notion that community efforts are needed to ensure that youth develop the resilience, knowledge, and abilities required to succeed in the modern world. We can apply this to digital literacy in that children cannot be taught digital literacy in a single lesson, by one instructor. Instead, distributing digital literacy across the curriculum is essential. Hague and Payton (2011) explained that developing digital literacy alongside subject areas is critical for preparing youth for a digital world. Youth use distributed and connected networks as a regular part of their lives.
>
> How do you apply distributed digital literacy in your school? Here are a few tips:
>
> - Meet with a tech coach or IT staff before teaching with technology to learn the best strategies and work out any issues in advance.
> - Share what you learn from teaching with technology with other teachers.
> - Feel confident to reach out to IT staff to alert them of problems students are having. For example, if a website that is needed for instruction is blocked, ask IT staff to consider adding it to the list of allowed sites.
> - Collaborate with the school librarian to include more information and media literacy in lessons. For example, the school librarian can give instruction sessions on how to find quality research for papers, write citations, and much more.
> - Allow students agency when using technology to create assignments. For example, instead of having students write a report, allow them to create media—a video, a podcast, a presentation, or other digital construction—to demonstrate learning.

Interdependence: Support for a Digital Learning Culture

What does a digital learning culture look like? Imagine a technology-rich classroom, where teachers and students are all tech-savvy, and equipped with the technology they need to be innovative and use technology to solve real-world problems. While such a learning environment is the goal, it takes time and hard work to reach. To make progress toward a culture like this, there must also be extensive support from administration in the form of time for both the teacher and student to innovate, funds to support the procurement of the latest equipment, and people to provide training and expertise on using it for teaching and learning. PBS Learning Media (2015) conducted a survey of teachers that found that teachers expected that the future of digital learning would require them to need more technology support, but also that they would be providing more technology support as well.

As such, building a digital learning culture requires interdependence. To advance digital literacy, a learning culture is possible only if technology users have the support needed to use technology. This support can come from many areas of the school. Administrators can provide funding for staff to provide technical support, like providing technology coaches and IT professionals. The technology staff can work closely with teachers to understand their needs and advocate for good policies, as well as teach teachers how to use technology for teaching or productivity. Teachers can support each other by sharing tips and techniques with each other. Teachers can also support students by taking time to model, mentor, or integrate technology into activities and assignments. This collaboration and network of caring is essential to developing a learning culture.

With an increase in school-issued devices comes new considerations for supporting the use of these devices, particularly remotely. Schools that switched quickly to 1:1 computing found they needed to provide digital training and more to staff and teachers, so they could in turn provide support to families who were using the devices. Klein reported how one school district had to train support staff in Spanish to support Spanish-speaking families who needed help learning to use the new devices their children brought home from school.

This poses the question: Can increased digital literacy reduce tech support needs? Many of the digital frameworks in use, including ISTE's Digital Skills for a Global

Society, focus on the skills needed to be an informed consumer, critical thinker, or creator. While these skills go beyond functionality, we argue that they are not possible unless technical skills are already present, for example, being technically literate enough to manage passwords, navigate websites, maintain a laptop, and manage device issues. A culture of digital literacy in a school would regularly examine the technical problems and concerns of using technology and create support for these issues. Support may include training, an FAQ page, a technical support phone and email address, policies designed to reduce problems with technology use, and walk-in help.

Incorporating the Simple Strategy of Building a Digital Culture

Now that we have considered the various types of culture building and reviewed examples, let's think about simple ways to implement these strategies:

> **CONNECTIONS: ISTE STANDARDS**
>
> **2.2 Leader.** Educators seek out opportunities for leadership to support student empowerment and success and to improve teaching and learning.

- Ask a colleague what digital skills their students are strong in—or low in.
- Start a conversation on what has worked to improve such skills or what might improve digital skills if the sky was the limit!
- Talk to support staff at your school to understand more about the problems parents are reporting related to technology used. Consider if there are ways to address these with instruction, or tutorials.
- Get to know your IT department and technology staff to understand how to request changes. For example, you might want to request changes to permit content that is erroneously being blocked in your classroom.
- Give a professional development session on a technology that you use to show others how it can improve teaching and learning. Leave room for discussion and ideas so that new ways of using it can emerge.
- Talk to your administrators about ways in which they can support your use of technology. Ask for what you need.

- Approach technology with a growth mindset. This excitement will spread to others!
- In Chapter 3, you started with yourself and determined the habits of mind that you use. Now, identify what habits of mind are used by others and consider opportunities for collaboration.

The Research

Although we feel strongly from our own personal experiences that a learning culture has the potential to make a positive impact on digital literacy in the classroom, there is more than just anecdotal evidence to support this practice. Here are some links to research labs working in this area:

- **The Media Education Lab.** The Media Education Lab is a research lab at the University of Rhode Island that specializes in research, advocacy, and mentoring of digital and media literacy in education. Hobbs and Coiro (2016) explained how collaboration and overlapping disciplines led to development of this lab and its subsequent Summer Institute in Digital Literacy, which brings together teachers, librarians, and media professionals to explore the practical implications of digital literacy. Scan the QR code to find more lesson plans on digital literacy at the Media Education Lab website (mediaeducationlab.com).

MEDIA EDUCATION LAB

- **The Connected Learning Lab.** The Connected Learning Lab is a research unit from the University of California, Irvine. Researchers study how youth can mobilize learning technology within a social network of mentors and peers so that they can eventually use technology to open opportunities. On the lab's website, you can find projects, research, and additional resources for using technology with youth to support their own interests, while also building relationships and opportunities (scan the QR code for more; connectedlearning.uci.edu/projects).

CONNECTED LEARNING LAB

Chapter 4 Takeaways

In this section, the important takeaways from the chapter are paired with the ISTE Standards for Educators that inform them.

- Advancing digital literacy requires utilizing the creative network of educators and staff who work to support teaching, learning and technology in schools (Collaborator 2.4.a).
- Sharing your use of technology and digital resources is a simple way to distribute digital literacy throughout the school and can help to support a shared vision of empowered learning (Leader 2.2.a, 2.2.c.).

Reflection

Before moving on, take some time to consider how the ideas in Chapter 4 apply within your context using the questions below.

- Who are the people who support digital literacy in your school?
- What problems could you solve by collaborating at different levels with other educators?
- Explore some of the research shared. Was there a school or classroom example that resonated with you? Why?

CHAPTER 5
Modeling Digital Literacy

KEY ISTE STANDARDS

This chapter addresses several ISTE Standards for Educators:

- Leader 2.2.c
- Citizen 2.3.a, 2.3.d
- Collaborator 2.4.d
- Facilitator 2.6.d

By the end of this chapter, you will:

- Recognize the different opportunities for modeling digital literacy.
- Describe strategies you can use to create opportunities for students to model digital literacy.
- Recognize digital skills that you already possess that can be modeled in the classroom.

What Is Modeling?

Students do as we do, not as we say, right? Modeling is a teaching strategy that is used for teaching content in all areas from science to writing. Modeling refers to how educators demonstrate new skills or expectations while they are teaching, with the intention of teaching that skill or expectation to students. For example, if you were teaching a learning technology, such as game-based learning to a group of adults, you might choose to incorporate Kahoot! (**kahoot.com**) into the presentation. Have them answer questions about your presentation and compete to win the game, rather than just showing them how to use its features. That way learners can authentically engage with the new skill, expectation, or resource as part of the learning process.

> **CONNECTIONS: ISTE STANDARDS**
>
> **2.3.a Citizen.** Create experiences for learners to make positive, socially responsible contributions and exhibit empathetic behavior online that build relationships and community.

Students can also model positive uses of technology for peers. Peer-to-peer learning can be teacher-led, such as using a jigsaw method (where students each become a specialist on using a technology, then teach it to others), or it can be organic and happen naturally among students (such as one student putting a cell phone on a charging station and in airplane mode, with others following for a cell-free learning space). A student who is using technology well for learning may also be asked to model their uses to the class. In doing so, students learn from peers but also increase content knowledge and improve their digital literacy skills as they incorporate data visualization, mind mapping, or even coding to create their models. Let's talk more about the different ways modeling can improve digital literacy!

Modeling: A Simple Strategy

Modeling is taught in teacher education programs as an instructional strategy. At its simplest, the teacher engages students by showing them how to perform a skill while describing it and providing a rationale. For instance, a teacher may model a common error that students make such as misspelling a word when searching for a book in the library catalog. Showing students the common error, its impact, and how to do the task correctly can help students when they are searching independently later. As an instructional approach, modeling often includes three components:

1. Conveying enjoyment or acceptance of something
2. Giving procedural guidelines to use something
3. Completing the task for others to see

For example, you can enthusiastically model a strategy by providing positive exclamations while performing the task (for example, a teacher might state while turning on a timer, "When I need to set aside uninterrupted time to focus, I set the timer on my phone for fifteen minutes to work"), or you can silently model by performing a task but not drawing attention to it. One example of this might be starting a Lofi Girl video to play on the screen while students work on homework to encourage focus time and model how to use media to create a relaxing work environment (see lofigirl.com to learn more). If you have ever been to a conference like ISTELive, then you have seen that vendors of educational technology often use enthusiastic modeling to explain the value of their product and how to use it. This is meant to encourage use and sell the product, but it also prepares the teacher with the skills they need to use it successfully.

Modeling can happen naturally as an event occurs; you seize the opportunity to model what you already do related to digital literacy to teach students, like allowing students to observe as you logout of an instructional session (thus promoting privacy and reminders to log out). We call this *teacher-led modeling*. Or, you can create opportunities for students to model for each other, which we call *student-led modeling*, like inviting students to participate in demonstrations. Within both categories of modeling, there are multiple strategies that you can apply in various contexts, as detailed in Table 5.1.

TABLE 5.1 Classification of Modeling Types from Select Literature

MODELING TYPE	DESCRIPTION
TEACHER-LED MODELING	
Silent modeling	Teachers use a tool in front of students without any explanation related to the tool.
Enthusiastic modeling	Teachers model use of a tool while making positive statements which demonstrate acceptance.
Simple exposure	Teachers intentionally make a tool available but do not use it.
Instructional modeling	Teachers explain how to use a tool while using it, much like a demonstration.
STUDENT-LED MODELING	
Silent peer modeling	Peers use a tool in front of each other.
Enthusiastic peer modeling	Peers (who are trained in the using the tool) model use of a tool while making positive statements that demonstrate acceptance.
Instructional peer modeling	Peers explain to each other how to use a tool while using it, much like a demonstration.
Self-modeling	Students use technology to observe themselves.
Expert modeling	Students look to experts to mimic practices or strategies.

Teacher-Led Modeling

Within a digital culture, educators who have mastered a tool can model it for others to use it too. Because we can't all be experts at everything, this mentorship plays a critical role in building a learning culture around digital literacy. The models that educators create around the technology they use are critical for how deeply learning occurs. Shannon McClintock Miller and William Bass reminded us in their book *Leading from the Library* that students need teachers as models. Even though they are born in the digital age, they need someone to share their digital lives and discuss how they make decisions regarding the technology that they choose to use. They wrote,

> It could be as simple as talking about why we, as adults, choose specific keywords for a search while you are making the search. In this case, we are simply modeling the decisions we make rather than assuming that our students will get it or respond to that one lesson plan where we discuss it. (McClintock Miller & Bass, 2019, p. 21)

In the classroom, modeling is often done through an *I Do, We Do, You Do* method (sometimes called *gradual release*). In this method, the teacher models a skill, then the full class does it, then students do it on their own. For technology, modeling is very important. This same strategy can be used when you are showing your fellow teachers a new tool you have been using or a feature that may be unique to others.

The I Do, We Do, You Do model is a research-based strategy designed to provide clear modeling and scaffolding to students (Fisher & Frey, 2008). It is designed to slowly release the responsibility from the teacher to the student, so that the student has more self-efficacy and autonomy to complete the activity on their own. Think about how you have learned technology in the past. For example, imagine attending a professional development session where the presenters use Slido (**slido.com**), an interactive software, in a professional development setting. The presenters use Slido to gather feedback from the attendees, so you get a chance to watch them use it and then try it yourself in a group setting. In addition, the presenters model how they are using Slido as an extension in their Google Slides presentation. Instead of just telling the attendees what to do, they take a few minutes to explain how they did it and show how to set it up. In addition, the presenters also model how Slido might best be used for engaging the class in discussion and invite discussion related to the quality of questions they asked, and how they might be improved.

Some technologies have features built in to facilitate using the modeling method and the I Do, We Do, You Do approach. For example, Nearpod (**nearpod.com**) shared a blog post (2023) that explained how teachers can use the student-paced presentations as a pre-test to gauge prior knowledge, then follow up by using Nearpod's whiteboard to model problems, processes, or vocabulary. In the We Do phase, teachers can use Nearpod's formative assessments, which may include drawings, polling, quizzing, or open-ended questions. Teachers should also be providing feedback in this phase as they see real-time results. Finally, in the You Do phase, Nearpod recommends its student-paced lesson delivery mode or to integrate other activities like PhET simulations (reseach-based online simulations of science and math concepts) or virtual reality (VR) field trips.

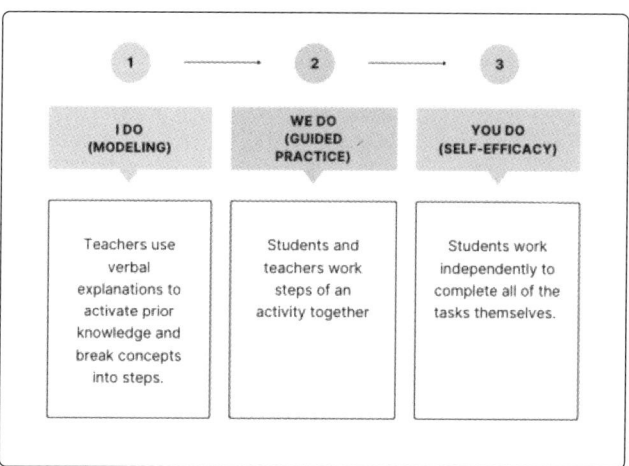

FIGURE 5.1
The I Do, We Do, You Do modeling technique

Some programs use virtual reality in combination with instructor modeling. For example, Munteen and Wallace (2023) explained that mechanical students in Maryland's Vehicles for Change program are learning how to work on vehicles by first watching an instructor demonstrate a skill, then they use virtual reality to practice the procedure themselves. Then students work through a checklist in VR before they try the procedure on a car.

Modeling isn't limited to the classroom. For example, a teacher might show a K–12 student how to do a search in Google to find the next book in a series. During library time, the student might then search in the library catalog for that title. The librarian can use this as an opportunity to model how to narrow a search using the catalog's faceted search features, so that the results include only books in a series. The results will also show where the item can be found in the library. The librarian can also show students how to click on subject headings to find more resources when the student is ready to read a new book outside of the series. Learning to use these features of the library catalog will help students as they use other databases in college and life, in addition to teaching them how to find the resources they need.

One way to think about modeling is to think about your own experience. Have you ever been in a workshop, and you needed the presenters to show you something, but instead they just talked about it? For example, a colleague told us about their experience in a workshop where attendees were learning about creating a digital portfolio, yet never saw an example of what a digital portfolio might look like. Hearing about the digital portfolio, without seeing it, hampered the learning process for our colleague. While it may not always be possible to show a finished product (for example, if you are teaching something new for the first time and do not have examples yet), taking time to model projects in development would also help.

Good modeling of digital literacy begins in the teacher education classroom during teacher preparation programs. In a study that examined how student teachers used technology, researchers discovered that student teachers were rarely considering digital inclusion when using technology (Kammer et al., 2023). Researchers recommended that teacher education faculties model digital inclusion in higher education classrooms, so that student teachers could then treat children in their classrooms the same way. In her educational technology course, Dr. Shantia Kerr Sims, a professor at the University of Central Missouri, models inclusion as a digital literacy strategy to prepare future technology educators to demonstrate flexibility when using technology. Kerr Sims (personal communication, March 27, 2023) said,

> *Students are asked to design and produce a variety of instructional materials. I redesigned this course last year to provide students more flexibility, autonomy, the opportunity for them to embrace their individual learning interests, and to account for varying levels of technology access. A large component of this specific course centers on student choice as well as the ability to create artifacts with their existing tools. For example, during one of the media assignments, students have the option to create an introductory podcast on a hosting platform or create a thorough plan for a self-published book, bringing it from conception to digital or in-person bookshelves. The book plan is submitted with a standard word processing software. Another instructional media activity gives the option to either create a slideshow, screencast, or Nearpod assignment. The purpose of the choices is twofold. One is to, again, give students choices on how they demonstrate their learning. The second reason is because during the pandemic, I found that without school access some of our students had very limited access to various technologies and high-speed internet connections. This course is taught over the summer, and with schools closed and travel some students still have limited access. This could cause problems viewing and creating streaming videos and other artifacts that require high internet service. For office hours I offer chat, phone calls, and video conferencing to ensure I can meet the needs of all students regardless of their access. All components of the course are made to address students' interest and their specific access.*

Kerr Sims modeled this for faculty and students at a professional development session in which she was a presenter, allowing faculty and pre-service teachers alike to learn more about using their own digital literacy to allow for inclusion, while also giving the students the freedom to develop digital literacy skills where they are comfortable. Table 5.2 explains how this strategy might be aligned with the Four Corners Framework.

TABLE 5.2 Alignment with the Four Corners Framework (Designer 2.5.a)

INTEGRATION	A professor of higher education wanted to model digital inclusion for students, who might one day become technology coaches or teachers using technology. Flexible and adaptable assignment submission was integrated into an existing assignment.
CULTURE	This professor had an opportunity to share this integration with other faculty and student teachers in a professional development session. By presenting on the use of free-choice for assessment, others were able to learn this and adapt their assignments as well.
MODELING	By integrating free-choice into assessments, the professor modeled how a teacher may do the same when teaching their classes.
MENTORSHIP	Students using free-choice for assessment would often interact online to share advice for how they were using different assessment tools, including both functional and critical digital skills.

In another example, sixth grade science teacher Tucker Judd uses modeling to teach students how to write emails. Though outside of the science curriculum, learning how to compose professional emails is a lifelong learning skill aligned with digital communication. For students who are used to texting and using brief written phrases, learning to write an email, and to check email for replies, is an important digital skill. To teach this, Judd provides feedback on the initial drafts for papers, emails them to students and asks the student to reply in email. Judd's instruction and initial email are used as models to demonstrate to students what an email should include.

Show Me!

The state of Missouri is known as the Show Me state. In the case of modeling digital literacy, "show me" can go a long way! Remembering that learners need teachers to "show me" increases student opportunities to see completed digital projects, demonstrations for using a technology, or examples of desirable behaviors when using technology.

A few simple ways that teachers can "show me" besides modeling during a live demonstration, might be to include an informative screenshot with lesson instructions that show steps needed to log in or use a technology or to create a quick video tutorial that demonstrates a technical process or strategy. Teachers can also provide a how-to worksheet instead of walking students through the steps of using a technology to allow students some autonomy when learning.

Student-Led Modeling

Teachers do not need to be responsible for all modeling that happens within a classroom. Students can engage in modeling too, and this can be showing others how to use a technology when they are using it. While I (Jenna) was observing high schoolers for a research study, one student told me how he showed another student how to get around internet filters to be able to watch a video for class. Though there is some deviance in this, his intentions were good, and it is an example of students showing other students how to do something related to technology. As a simple strategy, encouraging students to share what they know with each other can help to develop a culture of digital literacy and build confidence for students, while also improving digital literacy competence.

Peer Modeling

Peer modeling is the term often used in the literature to describe how students might influence one another to improve or change their use or understanding of something. Social cognitive theory suggests that students are very influenced by their peers and will often try something when they see others doing it too (Bandura, 1997).

For students, seeing how peers and others do something is an effective way to learn. Like teacher-led modeling, peer modeling can include silent modeling (a student does something that others observe) or enthusiastic modeling (the student verbally shares what they like about something or how they do it well). Students can also provide instructional modeling for peers by explaining how they did something.

In the wild, children do silent peer modeling to learn digital skills all the time. *Silent peer modeling* is the term that best describes the phenomenon of how students learn and improve their skills on social media. For example, when one teen uses a Snapchat filter, another will see the filter, find the name of the filter, and then use that same filter. They are not verbally sharing this information; it is happening silently yet encouraging adoption of new digital skills.

Self-Modeling

Technology also makes it possible for students to learn from themselves, including critiquing their own behaviors or style. For example, students can use self-modeling by recording themselves presenting, reading out loud, giving a speech, speaking another language, or any other activity for which self-review is helpful. In sports, teams often analyze videos of their games to understand more about what they did well or need to improve upon. Lang et al. (2009) also explained that video self-modeling worked as an intervention for young children on the autism spectrum. The children were told a classroom rule, then shown videos of themselves violating or following the rule. From rewatching these videos, in addition to instructional support, the students were able to model the desired behaviors.

Gaming may be another way to self-model. Students see themselves as the character, participating in different interactive environments. Certain games are especially good for self-modeling. For example, the Kai XR (kaixr.com) virtual reality teaching platform has lesson plans for K–12 learning that include an Aladdin game for developing skills in self-awareness, a career in illustration for self-management, and an NBA All-Star game to develop relationship skills (Frazier, 2022). (For more on games as part of an integrated digital literacy experience, see Chapter 3.)

Expert Modeling

Another form of modeling is teaching students to use experts as models. Copying a painter's masterwork is a traditional way for artists to learn their craft, and now computer science teachers and others who teach students to code are taking a similar approach. Students copy and paste existing code, and then modify that code to customize it. Experts describe this as a common way to learn coding; a more experienced person created the code and a new learner modifying it is essentially a case of modeling the code to become self-sufficient and self-reliant (Abraham, 2022). In a research study that analyzed the teaching strategies of computer science teachers, Hays and Kammer (2021b) found that several teachers used this type of expert modeling as a debugging exercise, such as viewing the source code of a Google Search box to create a customized search (Coding with Elias, 2021).

Could ChatGPT, an artificial intelligence tool, be considered an expert modeling tool for students? Maybe! At the time of this writing, educators around the world are discussing how ChatGPT will change teaching and learning. As a digital literacy concern, ChatGPT has its own opportunities. For example, a teacher may want to consider how to teach students to use ChatGPT for assistance with homework. Asking ChatGPT to provide a counter argument to a student's choice of topic could provide them with a starting point to analyze their own work for flaws, gaps or other missing elements. In addition, ChatGPT is known to be outdated and not always correct, which provides another opportunity for students to practice their evaluation skills. Roose (2023) explained that one English teacher taught students to use ChatGPT to create outlines comparing two short stories, then students used the outlines to write an essay. This encouraged students to use ChatGPT for assistance, but relied on the student to create the assessment and do the critical thinking.

A few other ways that ChatGPT (or future generative AI products) can be used for modeling may include:

- Asking ChatGPT to generate a draft of a five paragraph essay on a topic. Students can use the evaluation mindset to review the content for flaws, while also learning about the strengths and weaknesses of AI (such as its ability to "hallucinate" or make up content). They can also use the mindset of lifelong learning by using Microsoft Word's Comment and Track Changes features to edit and improve the content.
- Use teacher-led modeling to demonstrate how to talk to AI. Learning how to write a prompt for AI is expected to be an emerging digital literacy skill. Prompts need to be specific and ask for an output. In addition, model how to frame a prompt (for example, ask AI to act as a pirate), set the tone (for example, write a joke), and revise (ask AI to make it better if the first result is not desirable).

CONNECTIONS
Student-Created Models

Another type of student-led modeling is the activity of creating a model for others to see, which demonstrates learning. When students create models, an entirely new element of learning is taking place. Modeling instruction is particularly common in the fields of science, technology, engineering, and math (STEM). Malcolm Wells developed the modeling method of instruction in 1980s, which is a more formalized approach to modeling and is based on the inquiry model of teaching. The modeling method of instruction asks students to collaboratively solve a problem using the scientific inquiry process (Wells et al., 1995). In doing so, they use digital literacy skills related to critical thinking, finding information, and collaboration. Because the modeling form of instruction is a student-led, inquiry-based approach, opportunities for integrating digital literacy can be found throughout the cycle. Megowan-Romanowicz (2016) explained that classrooms that use modeling instruction perform better on measures than those in traditional classrooms because the students take the lead on solving problems, rather than passively learning in a lecture-based method. Instructors ask students to explain their thinking.

Through this inquiry process, students can conduct research to understand more about the problem they are investigating. They find examples in real life and cite them as evidence to support their own choices. At all stages, students are engaging in discussions and making sense of what they are learning by sharing and discussing their ideas in groups. To do this, they may construct graphs, draw diagrams, or use equations to model their thinking.

Modeling Habits of Mind

Habits of mind can be difficult to model because they are internal thought processes. Yet, students need to understand how to think about digital tools and digital skills. Therefore, start simple: Share your thoughts out loud as you walk through a task to model the habits of mind needed for digital literacy. For example, as you access a kahoot for students to play, you could say, "I selected Kahoot! because it is a tool that supports retrieval practice." Or you could say, "I am using my school credentials to log in to Kahoot! because it is connected to our single sign-on at the school."

Another example of how to model digital literacy habits of mind is when you are creating a document for students to collaborate on. Suppose, for example, you want students to give responses on Padlet (**padlet.com**). You quickly build the padlet in class while students wait. As you create the padlet, you can explain your steps and why each step is necessary.

Administrator-Led Modeling

Administrators play an important role in the development of teacher digital literacy and also support digital literacy initiatives in the school. Taking action to support digital initiatives is one way that administrators model the importance of digital literacy for the school community. Guiding strategies that administrators use to support teaching and learning with technology include:

> **CONNECTIONS: ISTE STANDARDS**
>
> **2.2.b Leader.** Advocate for equitable access to educational technology, digital content and learning opportunities to meet the diverse needs of all students.

- Providing professional development on leveraging learning technology, or providing time for teachers to seek their own professional development
- Creating incentives to innovate in digital pedagogy
- Supporting professional learning communities (PLCs) for digital pedagogy across grade levels, across content areas, or in areas of special interest
- Hiring full- or part-time technology coaches or staff to provide instructional support for teaching with technology
- Using technology for improvements in working conditions within the school, such as scheduling, communicating, or virtual meetings
- Securing funding for improved technology including learning management systems, single-sign-on technology, assistive technology, mobile technology for students and teachers, and digital information resources

Do the administrators in your school do any of these things? If not, do you feel comfortable asking or advocating for improved technology support to support student needs?

Incorporating the Simple Strategy of Modeling

Modeling is part of almost all the ISTE standards. Educators can model for colleagues, students, and parents. This chapter includes many ideas for modeling digital literacy. To model for digital literacy, teachers do not have to know the answer to all questions. For example, a student asks, "What is the happiest country in the world?" Instead of answering the question directly, say, "Let's find out together!" Then model how to find the answer in a fact-based resource by showing students how to search for the information. Explain what cues you see that indicate trustworthiness (or lack of!) of the source.

There are many other areas of digital learning that can include elements of digital literacy learning. The following areas to model are partially derived from Vicki Davis's "9 Key Ps" of digital citizenship (2014):

1. Creating secure **passwords**
2. Protecting **private** information
3. Carefully sharing **personal** information
4. Understanding the data gathered when taking a **photograph** (geotagging, facial recognition)
5. Respecting one's intellectual **property**
6. Getting **permission** to use others' work
7. **Protecting** devices and data from viruses, malware, phishing, identify theft, etc.
8. Using **professionalism** when writing online content in emails or social media
9. Creating a **personal** brand that represents yourself positively online

The 9 Key Ps can be modeled to teach digital literacy in the following ways:

- **Model digital etiquette.** Every online interaction with students is an opportunity for teachers to model digital etiquette. When sending emails, providing feedback, or creating content, use professionalism. Correct spelling, grammar, tone, greetings and closings, and polite language can be modeled to students. In addition, using communication features, like the Track Changes or Comment features in word processing software can demonstrate professionalism and functional use of these features for academic communication.

- **Model digital inclusion.** As a digital literacy skill, digital inclusion involves understanding how to accommodate others' diverse needs and being aware when technology is leaving others out. This can range from considering who to carbon copy on an email or add (or remove) to a chat group (social inclusion/exclusion) to using features of a technology, like enlarging text or using captions on media, that adapt to other learners' needs (assistive technology). In fact, using assistive technologies while teaching can normalize their use. Simply getting into the habit of using the Closed Captioning feature when showing video is a simple way to model digital inclusion, while also creating more acceptance within the classroom. Another tool which could easily be integrated into instruction, would be the Magnification tool which zooms in on text to enlarge it.

- **Model digital security.** Teachers make efforts to be safe online every day. For example, you wouldn't type a password while presenting your screen to the class. This type of practice can be modeled to students so that they understand why security is important. You can model other safety practices, such as checking to make sure a website is secure, as you use them. Remember, your school also implements security features, like single sign-on or content filters, which you can explain as you encounter them. Because these features impact who has access to information (for example, databases purchased by the school like Epic (**getepic.com**) or ProQuest (**proquest.com**) are for those with a school-issued email address only), passwords are an important part of digital literacy.

- **Model digital ownership.** Teachers often create instructional materials that are shared with the class. Sometimes you might use material that other teachers have created or publishers may have created. Noting who created the material, either verbally or by including full citations on slides or in handouts, is one way to model digital ownership and teach the digital literacy skill of understanding authorship. Teachers may also wish to include personal branding on instructional materials that they create and allow students to model this on the works that they create in class. Seeing this is helpful for students who are often creating and posting their own materials online. It also teaches students the mental habit of questioning to always consider who created an information resource (and why they might have created it).

- **Model digital equity.** Not everyone has the same access to technology. Schools that provide 1:1 programs (a mobile device for every student) are working toward increased digital equity. However, even if all students have a device that they can use in and out of the classroom, the device may break, the student may not have access to the internet, or it may lose functionality. Teachers can model digital equity in the classroom by understanding these issues as barriers to accessing information and considering how to solve them. For example, you could make a charging station available in class, give students reminders about device management and care, maintain an extra device in the classroom for emergencies, and clarify the rules and regulations for school-issued devices.

The Research

Although there has not been much research on modeling in digital literacy specifically, modeling as a teaching strategy is well-established. The following research explains how and why modeling might work as a simple strategy for teaching digital literacy.

- **The theory behind modeling.** Social cognitive theory (Bandura, 1997) suggests that modeling is an effective way to encourage students to accept new ideas and ways of thinking. While adult modeling is effective, Bandura suggested that peer modeling, which can include peers of the same age or older, more knowledgeable peers is even more effective (see Chapter 6 for more about mentoring).
- **Modeling success case studies.** The effectiveness of modeling as a teaching strategy has been examined in several cases within education research. Hendy and Raudenbush (2000) examined teacher modeling to encourage food acceptance in preschool children. They found that teachers felt modeling was the most effective teaching action, but that modeling needed to be enthusiastic (for example, "Yum, I love bananas") rather than silent. However, once students were exposed to peer modeling, children no longer responded to adult modeling.

    Methe and Hintze (2003) also examined the effectiveness of modeling, but as a teaching tool to increase student reading behavior. They found that when teachers modeled good reading behavior, including verbally describing how much they loved to read while also explaining how they create good habits for reading and reading while students were also engaging in silent reading, students also had high levels of on-task reading behavior.

- **Modeling with technology.** Teachers are social agents who influence their student's use of technology. Lai (2015) explored this by examining how teacher support influenced students' use of technology for self-directed language learning outside of the classroom. Lai found that when teachers provided encouragement, students were the most likely to use technology. However, self-directed use was even higher when teachers provided recommendations for using technology, guidance on how to use it, and demonstrations of how to use it in class.

Chapter 5 Takeaways

In this section, the important takeaways from the chapter are paired with the ISTE Standards for Educators that inform them.

- Model strategies that work for you by showing other teachers. In addition to talking about use of a technology, model technology use of digital literacy skills when the opportunities arise (Leader 2.2.c).
- Teachers can naturally use modeling as they are teaching by talking through their own actions and procedures. Because many teachers present on a screen or whiteboard, students view teachers' good practices and learn to use these same habits. This can be especially useful to teach good digital citizenship practices (Citizen 2.3.d).
- Modeling is an effective teaching strategy which has been in use for a long time and for teaching many different lessons and topics to enhance communication with students (Collaborator 2.4.d).
- Teachers can also intentionally design modeling into their lessons through approaches like the I Do, We Do, You Do approach, which leads students to self-efficacy and independence (Facilitator 2.6.d).

Reflection

Before moving on, take some time to consider how the ideas in Chapter 5 apply within your context using the questions below.

- What modeling strategies do you use for teaching?
- What digital skills could you model when you are teaching?
- How are administrators modeling digital literacy in your school or district?
- What opportunities are there for students to model digital literacy for others?

CHAPTER 6
Mentoring for Digital Literacy

KEY ISTE STANDARDS

This chapter addresses several ISTE Standards for Educators:

- Learner 2.1.b
- Leader 2.2.c
- Citizen 2.3.c
- Facilitator 2.6.d

By the end of this chapter, you will:

- Discover how to use mentoring to improve digital literacy in your students.
- Identify strategies you can use for mentoring in digital literacy.

Mentoring: A Simple Strategy

Mentoring is a strategy used widely in all levels of education. In fact, mentoring is "one of the most important strategies to support novices learning to teach" (Wang, 2001, p. 52). Pre-service teachers engage in a mentoring relationship with their cooperating teacher. Many new teachers are also assigned a mentor during the first year, and grade-level teams and professional learning networks can serve in the place of formal mentoring when teachers need to seek out new ideas or get feedback.

According to ISTE (2023), mentoring "refers to the ongoing coaching, facilitation, and support of learners" whether those learners are novice teachers or students. "In addition to modeling for students," ISTE continues, "we expect educators to demonstrate strategies to support students' development of skills. These could be but are not limited to integration into curriculum/assignments/assessments, re-teaching as needed, or one on one/small group support."

Because mentoring is already an integral part of education, using it for digital literacy growth is a natural step. While formal mentorship opportunities can be established for digital literacy, mentoring in digital literacy does not have to be an additional task; instead, it can be woven into existing relationships.

Let's consider the different ways mentoring in digital literacy could look. To start, Mullen and Klimaitis identified nine types of mentoring in education, as detailed in Table 6.1 (2021, p. 25).

TABLE 6.1 Classification of Mentoring Alternatives/Types in Select Literature

MENTORING TYPE	KEY ASSOCIATED DIMENSION
Formal mentoring	Planned programmatic interactions
Informal mentoring	Spontaneous mentor–mentee interactions
Diverse mentoring	Relationally mixed demographics and interests
Electronic mentoring	Interaction at a distance via technology
Co-mentoring/collaborative mentoring	Transformative relational development
Group mentoring	Shared agendas grounded in differences
Peer mentoring	Peer-based, empowering, helping relationship
Multilevel mentoring	Mentoring across organizational levels
Cultural mentoring	Diverse cultures united in mutual goals

Digital literacy can be woven into each of these mentoring types. Let's look at examples:

- **Formal mentoring:** Formal mentoring relationships can be established for the purposes of growing in digital literacy. This program could be established by the school administration, instructional coaches, or between pre-service teachers and faculty or cooperating teachers.
- **Informal mentoring:** Two individuals who both have an interest in digital literacy may organically form a mentoring relationship. These can be fostered through professional learning networks, grade-level teams, or subject-area teams.
- **Diverse mentoring:** This type of mentoring can be born out of opportunities that are facilitated across districts or across different areas of digital literacy. One teacher might have a specific interest in collaboration with digital tools, while another teacher's interest is digital information environments. The two teachers decide to work together because they think they can learn from each other.
- **Electronic mentoring:** Mentoring around digital literacy does not have to occur face to face. Instead, either formal or informal mentoring can be fostered through technology. Individuals can even meet through social media over a common interest in digital literacy and decide to expand their professional relationship.
- **Co-mentoring/collaborative mentoring:** The focus of this type of mentoring is two individuals who may possess different skills and knowledge about digital literacy but bring an equal amount of knowledge and experience to the mentoring relationship. A key element in co-mentoring/collaborative mentoring is the "dynamic partnership built upon reciprocity, despite differences in knowledge and expertise, and status and rank" (Mullen & Klimaitis, 2021, p. 27).
- **Group mentoring:** Groups can be created on the topic of digital literacy. Participants in the group can engage in mentoring as they share ideas, provide feedback, and support individual goals.
- **Peer mentoring:** Individuals engaged in this type of mentoring relationship are peers and both possess an interest in digital literacy. "The purpose of peer mentoring is to help foster a sense of belonging" (Mullen & Klimaitis, 2021, p. 28). For individuals who may feel they are alone in their interest in digital literacy, having a peer with a similar interest can help them remain focused and moving toward their goals.

- **Multilevel mentoring:** Districts can develop mentoring programs in digital literacy to align with institutional goals.
- **Cultural mentoring:** Cross-cultural relationships can be established around the topic of digital literacy. Professional organizations can create mentoring programs and partner educators from different cultural backgrounds for the purposes of expanding horizons and working toward equitable solutions for all students.

Research has shown that mentoring can be used successfully as a professional tool for digital literacy (Zimmer & Matthews, 2022). It is important to consider how the various types of mentoring can be used in your educational context. The goal with mentoring for digital literacy is to find a strategy that works best for you and potentially other teachers in your school.

Here's one simple idea: At the beginning of the year explain to your students that each quarter you will assign digital literacy partners. Digital literacy partners are meant to be supportive and should be each students' first point of contact when a question about technology arises. If both students cannot figure it out, then they should ask the teacher (you) or another student or partner group. Digital literacy partners can come together during assignments that require the use of technology, or you can arrange digital literacy partners next to each other for the quarter and make sure they are working on similar projects. Table 6.2 aligns this strategy with the Four Corners Framework.

TABLE 6.2 Alignment with the Four Corners Framework (Designer 2.5.a)

INTEGRATION	The classroom teacher starts the year by assigning digital literacy partners within the class.
CULTURE	The classroom teacher shares about the use of digital literacy partners at a team meeting. Other teachers are able to add digital literacy partners to their classes or call on students to pair up with their digital literacy partner when they work with that class.
MODELING	Digital literacy partners can model for each other how to use a technology. For example, if students created a graphic in an AI tool like DALL•E 2, partners can share with each other the prompt they used and make suggestions.
MENTORSHIP	Digital literacy partners can mentor other partner groups by teaching them what they have learned or what their partner group has been able to accomplish. The partner team can even mentor the teacher when something new is discovered.

Mentoring Between Educators

While mentoring in digital literacy can be woven into existing mentoring relationships, schools can also establish separate mentoring programs that are specific to digital literacy. The decision of how best to address digital literacy mentoring will vary from district to district, school to school, and perhaps even teacher to teacher. What we hope is that teachers and school administrators take time to discuss the state of digital literacy in their schools and develop ways to improve it together. To determine how best to improve digital literacy through mentorship, consider the following questions:

- What digital literacy strengths do students possess?
- What digital literacy strengths do teachers possess?
- In what areas do students have room for improvement in digital literacy?
- In what areas do teachers have room for improvement in digital literacy?
- What areas for improvement do we want to address first?
- How can mentoring support growth in the identified areas for improvement?
- What type of mentoring will be best?

The last question may be one of the more challenging to answer. When thinking about how to develop a mentoring program, it is important to spend plenty of time in the planning stage so that the program can be as successful as possible. Top et al. (2021) found that in a mentor/mentee program teachers wish to focus on their own interests and perceived needs instead of working through a formal curriculum. Talk to your colleagues about their needs and interests, then match mentors who can address those areas. For example, you could:

1. Survey teachers to see what type of mentoring they are interested in participating in.
2. Note any previous mentoring experiences teachers have and what worked well and what did not.
3. Consider time commitments and when teachers will participate in mentoring.
4. Identify champions of both digital literacy and mentoring. Ask them for their ideas and their help.

Once you have decided to use mentoring for digital literacy growth, speak with your champions of digital literacy who are also passionate about mentoring and ask them to share ideas and their enthusiasm with others. Identify how mentoring will help teachers grow their own digital literacy skills and in turn support students. Consider giving incentives for participating in mentoring. This will help mentoring in digital literacy feel more organic and less top down. It is important that participants in a mentoring relationship want to be mentored.

Giles et al. (2020) found a peer mentoring program increased pre-service teachers' proficiency with technology and motivated them. Although this study looked at education students and not teachers in the field, there is still valuable insight to be gleaned from the results: Peer mentoring can be motivating, and it can increase technology proficiency. Another result from this study that has implications for the development of mentoring programs is that 91% of the study participants preferred the teacher select their peer mentor instead of needing to select one themself.

> **CONNECTIONS: ISTE STANDARDS**
>
> **2.2.b Leader.** Advocate for equitable access to educational technology, digital content and learning opportunities to meet the diverse needs of all students.

Teachers Mentoring Students

Teachers also can mentor students in digital literacy. In many ways, teachers are always mentoring their students. However, we can make this more purposeful through the creation of after school clubs or student leadership groups that focus on digital literacy. These groups would be sponsored by a teacher and could focus on such topics as healthy technology habits, preparing for college and the workforce with technology, or a particular technology interest (e.g., digital writing club, digital art, and so on). For example, a film club sponsor may include a digital literacy–focused activity in which students view a film, then discuss and analyze the use of camera, characters, and color (referred to as 3Cs in filmmaking), or sound, story, and setting (referred to as 3Ss in filmmaking) to understand how these convey meaning, emotion, and messaging (to learn more, visit the Into Film website, **intofilm.org**).

As Palmer (2007) wrote,

> Mentors and apprentices are partners in an ancient human dance, and one of teaching's great rewards is the daily chance it gives us to get back on the dance floor. It is the dance of the spiraling generations, in which the old empower the young with their experience and the young empower the old with new life, reweaving the fabric of the human community as they touch and turn. (p. 26)

Students Mentoring Other Students

Students mentoring other students is often referred to as *peer mentoring*. Frequently, peer mentoring occurs across ages with an older youth mentoring a younger teenager or child. According to the Mentoring Resource Center (2008),

> Cross-age peer programs take advantage of adolescents' increasing interest in peer friendships as they enter the teenage years. Mentees' natural tendency to look up to slightly older youth means that they view their mentor as a role model and someone worth listening to. Peer mentors also benefit from interacting with each other in positive ways through the volunteer experience, often building new relationships beyond their normal circle of friends. (p. 1)

Because technology is so prevalent in the lives of today's students, providing opportunities for students to interact with older peers about the use of technology can be impactful.

Peer mentoring programs focused on digital literacy can come in many different forms. Here are a few ideas to get you started thinking about what this could look like in your educational context:

- Partner older students with younger students to work on a digital project.
- Assign a mixed age group of students to handle the school's social media channels for a week. This would need teacher oversight, but the students would work together to decide how to communicate ideas.
- Create a more traditional peer mentoring program where older students discuss with younger students about making decisions regarding their digital footprint and how they navigate life online.

Ryan Strutin, an instructional technology coach in Hong Kong, described to us how Canva (canva.com) can be used by students to create videos. Strutin (personal communication, December 13, 2022) said,

> *Video is a powerful medium that we all use to consume and create knowledge to share with an authentic audience, yet learning the skills to edit a video can take time—especially to create something of high quality. Canva is an online tool (free for schools) that simplifies video creation, and collaboration, enabling teachers and students to get started and build their digital literacy around creating video to communicate. Beyond simply editing their recording, students learn several skills when creating video together, including:*
>
> - *Independent and active learning*
> - *Differentiation*
> - *Real-world applications*
> - *Peer collaboration*
> - *Writing, speaking, and listening*
> - *Presentation skills*

While creating media, and sharing how they did it, students have the opportunity to mentor each other. Students will often inspire each other and be able to share how they did something with each other when they work together or present for each other. One simple strategy for increasing digital literacy with student-led mentoring is to allow students to present their student-created videos to each other with time to talk about what they did to create the video and write the content.

Students Mentoring Teachers

We often find that our students know things we do not know. There are also times when we have felt our students know more than we do about technology. While the concept of a digital native has been debunked (Kirschner & Bruyckere, 2017; see Chapter 1 for details about this research), what remains true is that today's students have grown up with technology and know a lot about digital tools that interest them. It is very likely that your students have spent a great deal more time on certain digital platforms than you have. Knowing this, we, as teachers, can learn a lot from our students.

At Iowa State University, for example, graduate students have been mentoring faculty for many years. The mentoring program was established to help faculty stay current with emerging technologies. Students are paired with faculty who match the needs and interests of the mentee and help the faculty to find the adequate technology to meet the next weeks learning goals. These students explore and recommend faculty use tools such as Flip (**info.flip.com**), Explain Everything (**explaineverything.com**), ClassDojo (**classdojo.com**), Makey Makey (**makeymakey.com**), Breakout EDU (**breakoutedu.com**), and more (Yu et al., 2018). This mentoring model of students mentoring their teachers is one that can be adapted for K–12. As we all know, it is hard to stay current on the technologies our students are using. By using a mentoring model like Iowa State's, teachers can gain insight into what technology tools their students are using, and students can gain skills in communication and collaboration. Students can also gain confidence as they work with teachers and other students to share their knowledge.

If you don't want to set up a formal mentoring program where students mentor teachers, you can certainly create opportunities where students share their knowledge, insights, and habits with you.

One thing you might learn as you listen to your students is how they manage and navigate technology in healthy ways. Encouraging students to share these practices can set a precedent that self-regulating technology use is an important skill to have and encourage. Without the opportunity to hear from our students about their habits there is no way we teachers can work to address healthy practices with families, the community, mental health professionals, and within the school. Therefore, taking time just to ask questions about technology use can be very valuable.

Despite unhealthy practices that are likely to be revealed, there are also going to be many amazing things students know how to do with technology that they want to share. Consider giving students the opportunity to participate in a technology show and tell. Students may explain how they record music, create digital art, write fan fiction, and more. Students may also want to share information about games they play and how they are successful playing the game. Additionally, students may share ways of communicating online that are entirely different than the experience you have as an adult. Students find sharing emotions with emojis is easier than using words (Zilka, 2021). At the same time, students have their own emoji vocabulary. For example, to a student, a skull emoji means something is funny (a figurative death) and a baseball cap means something is a lie (slang for *capping* which means to lie).

Another way students can mentor teachers in the use of technology, is for teachers to regularly ask their students to highlight new digital tools. For example, you could create an assignment where each week students submit a website they like to visit or submit a new feature they discovered on a digital tool they have been using for class. Students may submit a range of websites from their favorite shopping sites, to their favorite YouTubers' channels. As a show-and-tell exercise, students could share how they originally found the site, what they like about it, what they think the goals of the site are, and what improvements they would like to see.

Students can also be given the opportunity to lead a short professional development session for teachers. For example, some students may have become very proficient in using a video creation platform in one of their classes and instead of having a teacher lead the PD session, students showcase how they have been using the tool. For example, many students have expertise in creating short videos on TikTok or using Reels on Instagram. Instead of attending training, students have learned from watching what others do. This type of learning can be effective when observation is part of mentoring.

Mentoring Through Discussion Groups

Book clubs, discussion groups, or journal article clubs can be a great way to spark ideas and grow in digital literacy—as well as a way to engage in group mentoring. Teachers can suggest books, articles, or blog posts they want others to read. The group then reads the recommended resource and comes together to share ideas for how the information can be used in their teaching.

> **CONNECTIONS: ISTE STANDARDS**
>
> **2.1 Learner.** Educators continually improve their practice by learning from and with others and exploring proven and promising practices that leverage technology to improve student learning.

For example, in his dissertation, Friesem (2015) discussed a book study the teachers at Ocean Elementary participated in to grow their digital literacy skills. Together, the teachers read *Discovering Media Literacy: Digital Media and Popular Culture in Elementary School* (2013) by Renee Hobbs and David Cooper Moore. Discussion of the book during once monthly meetings "sparked many creative ideas from each and every one of the teachers" (Friesem, 2015, p. 263).

Discussions do not have to occur only amongst teachers in one building. In addition, teachers can use digital networks to stay current and remain in conversation about technology tools for digital literacy. These networks are often referred to as *professional learning networks* (PLNs) or *professional learning communities* (PLCs). No matter the name, the goal of the network/community is for teachers to gain new ideas and stay current.

After the release of ChatGPT in November of 2022, for example, many higher education faculty took to listservs (which are essentially email discussion groups) to share the many concerns, ideas, and opportunities they saw for this artificial intelligence (AI) tool. The conversations that occurred were examples of informal mentoring as faculty took the conversations offline to continue developing instruction that would use what AI has to offer. In addition to listserv conversations, many blog posts and tweets were posted. One excellent example is Derek Bruff's post "Three Things to Know about AI Tools and Teaching" on his blog *Agile Learning*.

Thinking about mentoring can be overwhelming, but if you can find a way to make it fit without adding a lot of extra work while also aligning it with existing interests and goals teachers have for themselves, then the chances of success are high. In the next section, we highlight a few ways mentoring can truly be simple.

Examples of Mentoring Aligned to Digital Literacy Skills

If you are interested in incorporating mentoring, it can be useful to reflect on what areas of digital literacy will best fit with digital literacy in your classroom. Consider these mentoring examples for the key skills ISTE identifies as necessary for digital literate individuals (**getdigitalskills.org**):

- **Locate information:** When sharing current events, ask students to include the site they visited, and how they determined the source was reliable (students mentoring students).
- **Evaluate sources:** Partner students and have them share the sources they are using for their research paper. Each student should explain to their partner their thought processes for determining credibility, bias, and influence (students mentoring students).

- **Interpret information:** Ask each student to bring an article to class about the topic you will be teaching. Have students share the articles and what perspective it is written from (students mentoring students).
- **Express ideas:** Students create a digital About Me using any software they like to use personally and then share it with the teacher. As part of the assignment, the students must share their favorite tips and tricks for the software (students mentoring teachers).
- **Communicate with others:** Teachers move their professional development to a virtual environment and share what they are learning and experiencing with their students (teachers mentoring teachers *and* teachers mentoring students).
- **Navigate technology ecosystems:** Teachers pick something from their past that is online and that they are comfortable sharing (e.g., high school track scores). This leads to a discussion about digital landscapes and digital footprints (teachers mentoring students).

Incorporating the Simple Strategy of Mentoring

Mentoring strategies can indeed be simple to implement. We hope the following examples will serve as idea generators.

- At the beginning of each day, take five minutes for a digital show and tell. Students share a digital tool (or resource) and explain how they use it, or they share digital work they created and explain their process.
- As part of a personal learning network, each day an instructional coach sends a tech tip for teachers.
- Teachers share the tech tip with their students. They ask students for their ideas on integrating the tip into learning.
- At the beginning of a new unit, teachers spend fifteen minutes explaining any new technology that will be used.
- At the beginning of a new unit, teachers take five minutes to highlight technology used in jobs related to the subject.
- At the end of the day, or class period, the teacher asks students for one content takeaway and one digital takeaway.

- Ask students to reflect on their mental thought processes when engaging with a technology tool. Ask them how they make decisions about what to click and how to use the tool. Then read through their reflections and provide feedback (mentoring) on their habits of mind.

Digital Literacy Mentoring Programs

In Chapter 2, we shared the different influences within a community that work together to influence digital literacy. One of these influences is community engagement. There are many examples of digital literacy mentoring programs outside of schools. These programs utilize the mentor-mentee model, assisting others to improve their digital literacy skills. Your students may be involved in these programs, or the programs possibly could become partners within the school.

- The Digital Literacy Foundation (**digitalliteracyus.org**) has an evidence-based mentoring program in which students work with a mentor to establish goals and to identify career paths related to digital literacy.
- The Latina Tech Mentor program (**missiongraduates.org/programs/parents/tech**) uses a mentorship model to connect Spanish-speaking tech mentors with parents in the community to facilitate the parents' development of technology skills.
- The Youngster.co program (**youngster.co**) is an intergenerational program in Australia that pairs teenagers with seniors. The teenagers mentor the seniors by providing technical help and digital life skills.

Public librarians can also serve as mentors in the community. In her article on digital mentorship for teens by information professionals, Samuel (2017) explained that public librarians have an opportunity to support digital literacy as young people use the library for personal and academic interests. She said,

> *On the one hand, young people benefit from mentoring that includes limit-setting as well as tech empowerment—that's exactly why mentor parents often dole out screen time limits along with tech lessons. On the other, young people who encounter mentors at their local library or media centre are also experiencing their first points of contact with public institutions and media; in this respect, information professionals have a unique role in teaching young people what they can and should expect as online citizens. That means their engagement with young patrons must ultimately be guided more by e pluribus unum than by in loco parentis.*

The Research

Mentoring is well established as an effective strategy for training and development in youth, academics, and the workplace. Here are some examples from the research.

- **Mentoring for teachers.** In their article "Toward a Conceptualization of Mentoring," one of the most cited works on mentoring in education (cited over 1,000 times), Anderson and Shannon (1988) explained that the main functions of mentoring are to teach (including modeling, informing, and questioning), sponsor (including protecting, supporting, and promoting), encourage (including affirming, inspiring, and challenging), counsel (including listening, probing, clarifying, and advising), and befriend (including accepting and relating). For new teachers, a mentoring program is helpful in building relationships if the relationship can capture many of these functions.

- **Technology mentors.** The role of the technology or instructional coach in schools (an embedded and sustained form of professional development for teachers) is an example of a contemporary mentoring program which is backed by research within the area of technology-media mentoring (Bakhshaei et al., 2020; Ertmer & Ottenbreit-Leftwich, 2013; Gentry et al., 2008; James, 2011; Knight, 2007). Section 4 of the ISTE Standards, Coaches, highlights the role of the coach as a mentor by explaining how technology and instructional coaches support, coach, model, and build relationships with teachers (ISTE, 2023).

Chapter 6 Takeaways

In this section, the important takeaways from the chapter are paired with the ISTE Standards for Educators that inform them.

- Mentoring is a simple strategy for growing in digital literacy. (Leader 2.2.c; Facilitator 2.6.d).
- Mentoring can take on many forms. It is important to determine what will work best in your educational context. Consider:
  - Mentoring between educators (Leader 2.2.c)
  - Teachers mentoring students (Citizen 2.3.c)
  - Students mentoring other students (Facilitator 2.6.a)
  - Students mentoring teachers (Learner 2.1.b)

Reflection

Before moving on, take some time to consider how the ideas in Chapter 6 apply within your context using the questions below.

- Revisit the seven questions related to developing a digital literacy mentoring program in the "Mentoring Between Educators" section. Is there anything you would change or add to that list of questions? How do you see those questions guiding the development of a digital mentoring program?
- What type of mentoring program do you see working best in your school?
- How would you set up a peer mentoring program on digital literacy?
- What ideas do you have for how students can mentor teachers in digital literacy?
- What mentoring example resonated with you? Why?

CHAPTER 7
Simple Digital Literacy Strategies Across the Curriculum

KEY ISTE STANDARDS

This chapter addresses several ISTE Standards for Educators:

- Citizen 2.3.a, 2.3.b, 2.3.c
- Designer 2.5.a, 2.5.b
- Facilitator 2.6.a, 2.6.b, 2.6.d

By the end of this chapter, you will:

- Review examples from educators from various locations and in various settings to see how they simply teach digital literacy.
- Align simple strategies with the Four Corners Framework to identify the greater impact.

Digital Literacy Case Studies

In this chapter, educators share how they integrated digital literacy into their content areas using simple strategies. Each educator was asked to share the problem they were having related to digital literacy, the solution they found to improve it, and the results they saw as students learned new digital skills. The following is an expert collection of stories ranging from an elementary school library to a high school Latin classroom to the strategies imparted in a pre-service teachers classroom. In their own words, educators explain the ages they serve, the strategies they use, the tools they use, and how they apply the ISTE Digital Skills. Each case study ends with a table that correlates the Four Corners Framework (Figure 7.1) with the strategy, pointing out how the simple actions are making a larger impact in the digital literacy of the school community. We hope that these stories inspire you to try something new to address digital literacy gaps in your classroom, or to work with intention on the digital literacy strategies you may already be using.

FIGURE 7.1
The Four Corners Framework for developing digital literacy in students

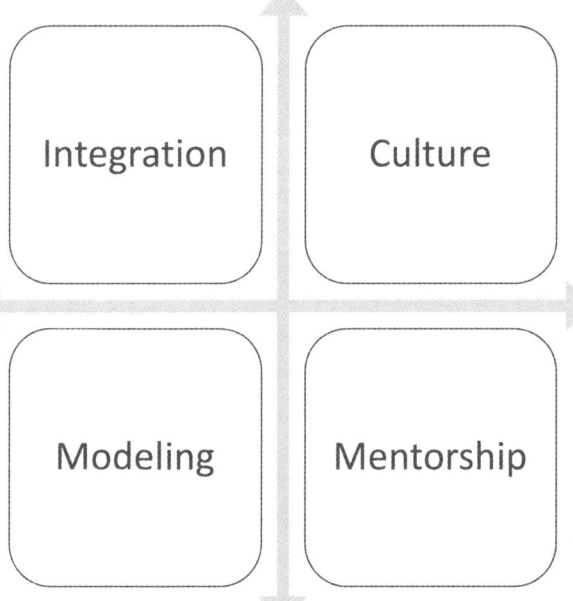

CASE STUDY 1
Analyzing News and Media Sources

My (Megan's) favorite way to teach multiple digital literacy skills at one time is to teach my students how to use the Media Analyzer (Figure 7.2) graphic organizer to evaluate websites for accuracy, quality, and legitimacy. I designed the Media Analyzer to help students critically consider a variety of aspects of the media or news source. Although I teach this as a lesson during ELA, students can apply the skills learned throughout all aspects of the day. For example, students can analyze the quality and validity of a digital resource used when researching the American Revolution in social studies or judge the accuracy and trustworthiness of a news article read on the Newsela website.

PROGRAM INFORMATION

GRADE LEVEL:
5th grade
SUBJECT AREA:
English Language Arts
LESSON AUTHOR:
Megan Mallon
LOCATION:
Manhattan, Kansas
ISTE DIGITAL SKILLS:
Locate information, evaluate sources
ISTE STANDARD FOR EDUCATORS:
Citizen 2.3.b
TECHNOLOGY TOOLS INTEGRATED:
Newsela (newsela.com)

This strategy focuses primarily on a specific branch of digital literacy: media literacy. When using this strategy, students can discuss, investigate, and apply a knowledge of several other digital literacy skills, including, but not limited to digital research skills, finding and consuming digital content (Tinmaz et al., 2022b), and digital fluency (Ribble, 2017). According to ISTE (n.d.), students need to be able to locate information in a digital format, while also being able to evaluate those sources and interpret the information found. When students learn how to use the Media Analyzer to evaluate a news or media source, they are incorporating all these skills.

In the last several years, more and more emphasis has been put on "fake news." The importance of teaching students how to navigate information online is more important than ever. As Pilgrim and Vasinda (2021) found, most students conduct research on specific, pre-approved websites given to them by their teacher. I believe it is important to teach elementary students how to find and evaluate websites on their own. This is a skill that is necessary both inside the classroom and out.

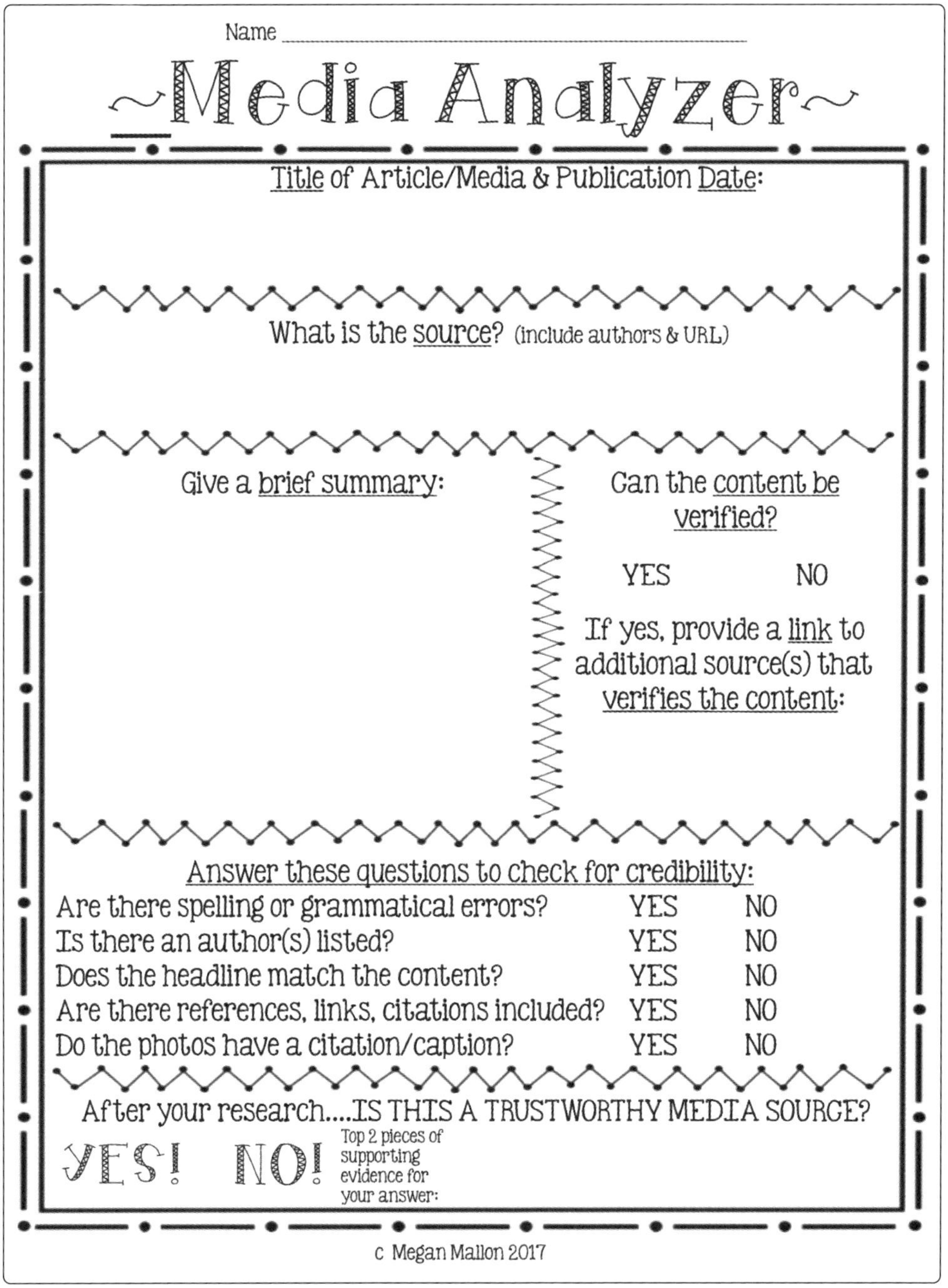

~Media Analyzer~

Name _____

Title of Article/Media & Publication **Date:**

What is the **source**? (include authors & URL)

Give a **brief summary**:

Can the **content be verified?**

YES   NO

If yes, provide a **link** to additional source(s) that **verifies the content:**

Answer these questions to check for credibility:

Are there spelling or grammatical errors?	YES	NO
Is there an author(s) listed?	YES	NO
Does the headline match the content?	YES	NO
Are there references, links, citations included?	YES	NO
Do the photos have a citation/caption?	YES	NO

After your research.....IS THIS A TRUSTWORTHY MEDIA SOURCE?

YES!   NO!

Top 2 pieces of supporting evidence for your answer:

c Megan Mallon 2017

FIGURE 7.2 Megan Mallon designed the Media Analyzer graphic organizer to help students evaluate sources for accuracy and legitimacy.

With this strategy, I first share with students an infographic (Kirschenbaum, 2017a) that outlines several aspects to look for when evaluating a website or news article for accuracy, quality, and legitimacy. This infographic helps students identify a variety of aspects to assess. For example, students might do a separate search on the author's last name or attempt to find other websites that discuss the same topic so they can compare the information. They may also want to look for quotes or statistics listed in the original source and attempt to verify those facts on another site. After discussing these elements with the students, I then share a website that was, unbeknownst to the students, created for the purpose of helping students identify factually inaccurate media. Kirschenbaum (2017b) has curated a list of several websites such as this, and my fifth graders especially enjoy the one dedicated to the Pacific Northwest Tree Octopus (Zapato, 1998).

Finally, I introduce the Media Analyzer to encourage students to think critically about the media they are consuming. The students fill out this graphic organizer with information garnered from the source. Students include the title and publication date of the source; this helps the learners realize the concerns with using outdated materials, especially when working with current events. Students must also give a summary of the source and work to verify the content through another source. Students then answer a variety of questions to check for credibility, such as the following:

- Are there any errors?
- Is an author listed?
- Does the headline match the content?
- Are there references, links, and citations included?
- Do the photos have a citation/caption?

After using the Media Analyzer, students should then be able to decide if the news or media source should be used. The goal is that, eventually, students will think through these aspects on their own without the help of the Media Analyzer.

This has been a very successful way of both introducing students to digital literacy skills and encouraging them to think critically about the news and media that they are consuming. Not only has it been successful, but it is fun and engaging for the students! They enjoy the aspect of analyzing the "fake" websites, especially because some of the facts included are preposterous, and there is not much that a fifth grader loves more than preposterous facts. The impact of this lesson can be seen again and again throughout the year. In an upper elementary classroom, we do a lot of research in a variety of content areas, and students have been known to say, "I don't think this website is accurate! Look what happened when I did a little research on the author!" or "I see at least three spelling errors in this paragraph. I don't think I want to use this website for my research information." Beyond the use in the classroom, it is also my hope that students will transfer these digital literacy skills to their lives at home, and hopefully teach their families the importance of analyzing the digital media they are consuming.

This case can be expanded to align with the strategies in Four Corners Framework, as Table 7.1 demonstrates.

TABLE 7.1 Case Study 1: Alignment with the Four Corners Framework

INTEGRATION	The teacher first determined what digital skills needed development and created the Media Analyzer sheet to encourage students to think through these steps.
CULTURE	One of the goals of this activity is to bridge the gap between school-provided information and encountering information while at home or independently searching. This involves students using these same skills outside of the classroom.
MODELING	In this example of enthusiastic modeling, the teacher shares the Media Analyzer sheet explaining how helpful it is for evaluating websites like The Endangered Pacific Northwest Tree Octopus site to determine legitimacy.
MENTORSHIP	Through peer mentorship, students can talk to each other about accuracy of information sources, sharing the strategies that they have learned with others.

CASE STUDY 2
Flattening the Latin Word

It used to be the case that students would memorize forms of words in Latin—more than 132 forms of every verb and 14 forms for every noun. Then they would apply their knowledge of the form of the word to help them translate a Latin sentence or paragraph. But in the last few years, a lot of tools have appeared that can parse the grammar behind every word, and students have been less and less inclined to put in the time and effort at memorization (which was effective for only a small subset of students anyway). So, I (Benjamin) have started directing my students to these resources as an intentional instructional practice. One good resource is wiktionary.org: Students can type any word in (say, *bellis*), and Wiktionary will tell them all of the possible forms for the word.

> **PROGRAM INFORMATION**
> **GRADE LEVEL:**
> 9th–12th grade
> **SUBJECT AREA:**
> Latin (foreign language)
> **LESSON AUTHOR:**
> Benjamin Johnson
> **LOCATION:**
> Hampden, Maine
> **ISTE DIGITAL SKILLS:**
> Locate information, interpret information
> **ISTE STANDARD FOR EDUCATORS:**
> Citizen 2.3.b
> **TECHNOLOGY TOOLS INTEGRATED:**
> Wiktionary (wiktionary.org)

Wiktionary is on an approved list of resources that I give to my students to use. With a whole lot of language resources out there now that I *don't* want them to use (e.g., Google Translate, AI tools), I feel that having teacher-approved resources helps relieve some of the pressure that my students feel around outside resources. I post these resources on our Google Classroom, my school's learning management system, and the results of their research are a constant topic of conversation.

I was seeing students struggling with the complex task of dealing with individual words in a story more and more. If a word doesn't quite make sense in the general backbone of the sentence (i.e., it's not in a prepositional phrase or as the subject or object of the verb). These stand-alone words can be hard, because students need to:

1. Figure out what the word means.
2. Understand what its syntax is.
3. Apply the knowledge of its syntax to help with a translation or comprehension of the sentence.

Using an online resource like Wiktionary helps flatten this multi-step process by addressing steps 1 and 2, which are both essentially low-level cognitive tasks, and allowing my students to focus on the application process.

I am finding that I can help more students by focusing on the harder parts of the language (application), while finding a fix for shortcomings that are becoming more and more prevalent (the lowered emphasis on memory and studying in schools has made it harder to expect students to have information in their heads to work with). It has also given students the tools they need to work through their issues on their own. They have fewer steps to progress through, which means fewer steps to trip them up, and fewer things they really need to know. This has led to more success, more of a feeling of success among my students, and more time to work with other cognitively difficult tasks.

I do wonder if some language learning, especially learning ancient languages, will continue down this path. I believe Tufts University is experimenting with an introductory Ancient Greek class that forgoes traditional language instruction in favor of something that assumes the wealth of syntax and vocabulary information and teaches students how to work with the information. In other words, assuming, especially in the beginning levels of the language, that you have access to tools that past generations of students never had, and then working slowly to wean students off these tools as they master more parts of the language.

The key here, though, is to use this as an intermediary step toward greater reading fluency in Latin (or Greek), rather than a necessary tool, without which people, regardless of their skill level, would be helpless.

This case can be expanded to align with the strategies in Four Corners, as Table 7.2 demonstrates.

TABLE 7.2 Case Study 2: Alignment with the Four Corners Framework

INTEGRATION	The teacher realized there was a gap in learning in that students were using sources like Google Translate, which provided inaccurate information.
CULTURE	This lesson extends outside of the school into the digital culture in the professional learning network for the teacher. As other educators share the problems and solutions related to language learning, a digital culture is developed.
MODELING	The teacher uses instructional modeling to show students how to use the desired tool, over tools they may be using on their own. This way, students use it correctly and with better accuracy. In addition, the teacher created a list of approved resources which he was comfortable with students using, modeling acceptance of these sources.
MENTORSHIP	The teacher provides teacher-student mentorship by helping them with deeper learning issues, once they can use technology to solve small issues on their own. This leads to increased self-efficacy for students and is more satisfying for the teacher who can focus on content-related questions.

CASE STUDY 3
AI or Human (Expert)

As we learn more about ChatGPT and generative AI in general, it becomes clear that AI is going to be a fixture in schools moving forward. Though tools like ChatGPT may soon be filtered from schools or become subscription based (for example, many AI programs have a Pro version that offers greater access), generative AI in some form will likely still be used in the classroom. Our (Jenna and Lauren) simple strategy is adapted from the *AI or Human* game (ai-or-human.github.io). In the original game, players view a photo and then choose if they think it was generated by AI or is a photograph of a real human. They must look for clues within the photo such as abnormal proportions, coloring,

PROGRAM INFORMATION

GRADE LEVEL:
9th–12th grade
SUBJECT AREA:
English Language Arts
LESSON AUTHORS:
Jenna Kammer and Lauren Hays
LOCATION:
Warrensburg, Missouri
ISTE DIGITAL SKILLS:
Interpret information, evaluate sources
ISTE STANDARD FOR EDUCATORS:
Citizen 2.3.c
TECHNOLOGY TOOLS INTEGRATED:
ChatGPT or found examples

patterns, lack of detail, or unrealistic imagery. At the same time, this helps players to practice their evaluation skills and use the mental habit of situated learning as they think about what AI can do and how it can appear as real.

In our version of the game, we use text instead of images. As a brain break, prepare some text in advance. For example, you could prompt AI to generate a poem about modern-day issues in the style of Emily Dickinson (a nineteenth-century poet), Amanda Gorman (a modern-day poet), or a poet who is studied in class. Show it to students and ask them to determine if it was written by AI or a human. While they are guessing, ask them to share clues that informed their choice. Encourage students to explain their reasoning with examples. Allow them to use devices to search for original works or to run the poem through an AI detector. The simple strategy can conclude with a discussion on what AI can or cannot do, and how AI detection related to literary works can or cannot be done. You could also use this strategy with product reviews (which are often generated by AI), tweets, or chunks of code—whatever works best for your subject area.

Taking time to discuss what AI can do, as well as its potential strengths and weaknesses, can help to prepare students with a mindset for situated learning (i.e., content generated by AI), as well as to think critically about media they consume.

This case can be expanded to align with the strategies in Four Corners, as Table 7.3 demonstrates.

TABLE 7.3 Case Study 3: Alignment with the Four Corners Framework

INTEGRATION	Teachers identify an area in their content where AI is able to generate works. The teacher finds examples of AI content (or real content).
CULTURE	Students begin to critically think about AI in other classes as well, maybe using AI to generate works or to discuss AI's ability to change the way things are currently being done in class.
MODELING	In this simple strategy, AI is modeling work. AI is using large data sets to create a model of a poem, product review, or essay. Teachers can discuss how this content is different from human-created content.
MENTORSHIP	As the conversation grows, students will likely mentor teachers on their uses and ideas for generative AI. They will have also developed strategies within their social groups for identifying AI-generated content, particulary imagery. Teachers can mentor each other on identifying AI-generated text, as well as strategies for detecting it when students use it.

CASE STUDY 4
Making the Case for Photo Credits

As an innovation specialist my (Tiffany's) role is to quite literally… be innovative! Innovation specialists at Lakota Local Schools are a two-for-one deal: part instructional coach and part technology integrationist. We work in specific buildings, but we often collaborate at the district level (K–12) too. Working with junior high teachers and students at the building level, I support teacher learning with best instructional practices and best technology integration practices, as well as help them create unique personalized learning experiences for students.

> **PROGRAM INFORMATION**
> **GRADE LEVEL:**
> 7th & 8th grade
> **SUBJECT AREA:**
> All
> **LESSON AUTHOR:**
> Tiffany Rexhausen
> **LOCATION:**
> Kansas, Ohio
> **ISTE DIGITAL SKILLS:**
> Locate information, express ideas
> **ISTE STANDARD FOR EDUCATORS:**
> Citizen 2.3 c
> **TECHNOLOGY TOOLS INTEGRATED:**
> Adobe Express (adobe.com/express)

While a good portion of my time is spent working alongside teachers, I also find ways to engage with students regularly. For example, I make sure that all students visit our Innovation Hub once a quarter during their Academic Support class periods (which is like a study hall bell with teacher supports). During this time, I teach students various skills or provide tutorials on technology tools that would support learning across the curriculum. Ultimately, my goal is not only to teach students skills and tools, but to also integrate digital wellness.

A good example of this is how my hands-on lesson about creating a web page using Adobe Express grew into a lesson on copyright awareness. The initial purpose of the activity was to provide students with another tool in their tool kits for project creation. Many of our teachers offer choices for project design, so I wanted students to see web page creation as one of those options. In addition, one of our teaching teams uses Adobe Express for students to create web pages during a project-based learning career unit, so my lesson provided those students with frontloading on the tool.

To start, students gave me ideas for a web page while we created one together. I modeled the process and options they have in Adobe Express throughout that portion of the lesson. Then they worked on their own to create web pages on any topic of their choice while I walked around and provided on-the-spot support. The lesson ended with a short share out of some of their web page creations.

During the lesson, I took the opportunity to discuss the importance of respecting copyrights. First, we talked about using the stock photos provided by Adobe Express versus inserting pictures found with Google. Then I showed students how Adobe credits the photos at the bottom of the finished web page, very similarly to how they would include a "Works Cited" page and credit the research and quotes they used in a piece of writing. They had already learned that they cannot include quotes from another source without giving credit to that source. Photos are no different. I provided another analogy by talking about music because many students know they cannot share music online because of licensing and copyright. Using some of their prior knowledge to connect the idea of needing permission for photos helped them understand that taking images from the internet isn't a free for all any more than using research with quotes or sharing music is.

I also demonstrated how to filter Google image searches so that Google will return only results that are licensed for reuse (Figure 7.3), in case students decided against going with the Adobe Express stock photos. (Jennifer Gonzalez wrote a great blog post on this for *Cult of Pedagogy*, called "Teaching Students to Legally Use Images Online" [2017].)

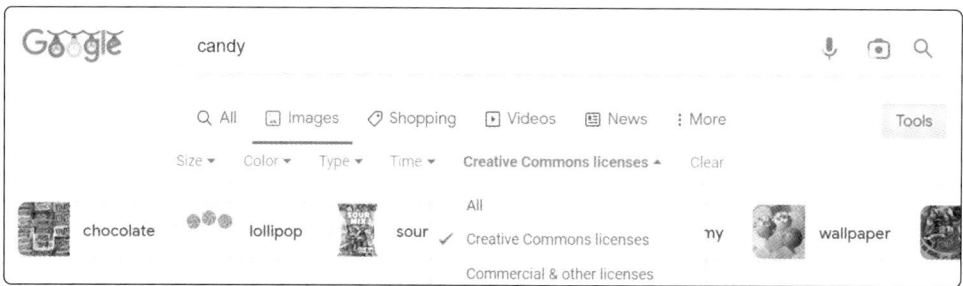

FIGURE 7.3 Filtering images by license type in a Google search

We eventually got into a conversation about copyright and right to use, so students would know how they can use that process to protect their own images. As their curiosity grew about how to copyright their own images, we dug a little deeper and did a quick Google search to learn about this process. The article "How to Copyright a Photograph or Image" (Kaminsky, 2023) on Legalzoom.com provided an overview of the process, including a checklist to see if an image qualifies for protection and a link to the application and filing fees.

The key ISTE Digital Skills addressed by the Innovation Hub activity were to help students learn to effectively locate content and express ideas. Being responsible digital citizens, students worked on locating content and using it responsibly as they expressed their ideas via web page creation. Helping students understand right-to-use issues and making sure they don't use photos incorrectly (without permission) is a key part of supporting their digital wellness. The same lesson applies to understanding their own rights as they create content online, so they know how to protect their images going forward. Students also learned how to cite sources for images using the Adobe Express version as a model, extending their knowledge of citing sources beyond typical research and quotes.

After learning more about usage rights for images, students often come to me to double-check if a photo is one they can use. Prior to the Innovation Hub lesson, most of them had no idea that photos and images could even be owned or that they needed permission to take images from the internet. I now teach this lesson with all students in our building at the beginning of the school year, and based on the number of the credits from Adobe Express stock photos I see at the bottom of their pages at the end of the year, it's a lesson in digital citizenship that sticks with them.

Throughout the year I try to embed some of these strategies when I am working with classes on other types of activities, such as research projects or learning a tech tool. If students have questions or need support, they can come to my room or our Innovation Hub where I can provide them with troubleshooting, quick tutorials, and some small nuggets of digital citizenship that correlates with their project or learning activity.

This case can be expanded to align with the strategies in Four Corners Framework, as Table 7.4 demonstrates.

TABLE 7.4 Case Study 4: Alignment with the Four Corners Framework

INTEGRATION	Students were unaware that images could be owned or required permission to use. Integrating instruction helped to make them more aware of usage rights.
CULTURE	The Innovation Hub serves as a support for the student body who have questions related to this topic.
MODELING	This strategy includes instructor modeling to show students where Adobe provides creator information and how to cite that properly.
MENTORSHIP	The specialist provides mentoring for students in the Innovation Hub.

CASE STUDY 5
The Digital Tattoo Strategy

To drive home the point with my students that whatever they share on the internet stays on the internet, I (Andrea) use the Digital Tattoo strategy. When discussing the permanency of content on the internet, the term often used is *digital footprint*. However, many educators feel the concept of a footprint is not permanent enough, but the term *tattoo* emphasizes the durability of content posted online (Cooper, 2016). Students know that when a tattoo is on someone's body, that it is permanent. This is something that they can see and understand with the naked eye. This strategy makes the concept of internet permanancy real for them, and it is quite simple:

PROGRAM INFORMATION

GRADE LEVEL:
6th–8th grade
SUBJECT AREA:
All
LESSON AUTHOR:
Andrea Cook
LOCATION:
Kansas City, Missouri
ISTE DIGITAL SKILLS:
Navigate technology ecosystems
ISTE STANDARD FOR EDUCATORS:
Citizen 2.3.d
TECHNOLOGY TOOLS INTEGRATED:
Internet Archive (archive.org), social media sites

1. Discus how a tattoo is permanent.
2. Compare a tattoo to what is posted online.
3. Show examples of digital tattoos (old social media posts, Internet Archive, old news stories).

4. Discuss the impact of content tattooed online.
5. Ask students to identify what they want tattooed on the internet.
6. Ask students to consider what they do *not* want tattooed on the internet.
7. Ask students to list what things they should not tattoo online about others.

I decided to use this strategy when I began to see an uptick of students using social media. Students were not allowed to use social media in the classroom; however, that did not stop some of the problems that would arise when social media was not used with good intentions. Sharing the Digital Tattoo strategy gave students the information needed to make an informed decision before sharing something that could affect their future.

Although I could not measure how well this strategy worked outside of the classroom, I do recall students understanding the strategy and its purpose. When hallway chatter during passing periods turned into middle school drama, I would gently remind students, once they entered the classroom and were settled, how important it was to think before sharing anything online that could be hurtful to themselves or someone else.

This case can be expanded to align with the strategies in Four Corners Framework, as Table 7.5 demonstrates.

TABLE 7.5 Case Study 5: Alignment with the Four Corners Framework

INTEGRATION	The teacher saw a gap when noticing that students were increasingly using social media. Using her own experience with social media, the teacher integrated a strategy to address it.
CULTURE	Once problems from social media made their way to the classroom, the teacher identified that was an area she had experience with and could share.
MODELING	The teacher used verbal modeling to guide students to using social media in healthy ways.
MENTORSHIP	Serving as a mentor for students, this teacher reminded students of the permanence of social media, with guidance for thinking before doing something that could be harmful and long-lasting.

CASE STUDY 6
Navigating Databases with Digital Breadcrumbs

The simple strategy that I (Matt) use with students is to pair children's literature with teaching students about navigating databases. In our school, all classes use PebbleGo, a database for beginning researchers that includes text, photos, and media on such topics as animals, science, biographies, social studies, and health. PebbleGo is adaptable by reading level and offers resources for teachers as well. Students need to learn how to use a database like this so they can find what they need. Teaching students how to research in PebbleGo is helpful for learning about many digital literacy topics, like navigation, citing sources, and finding information, as well.

PROGRAM INFORMATION

GRADE LEVEL:
K–5th grade
SUBJECT AREA:
Library
LESSON AUTHOR:
Matt King
LOCATION:
St. Louis, Missouri
ISTE DIGITAL SKILLS:
Navigate technology ecosystems
ISTE STANDARD FOR EDUCATORS:
Citizen 2.3.b
TECHNOLOGY TOOLS INTEGRATED:
PebbleGo (pebblego.com)

With my simple strategy, I teach students how to use the main navigation features of PebbleGo so they can understand more about the organization and structure of the database. First, I read aloud a rendition of the fairy tale *Hansel and Gretel*, which is the story of how two siblings lay a trail of breadcrumbs as they venture into the woods so they can find their way home. Next, I project PebbleGo on a whiteboard so the students can watch what I do as we complete a guided search together. We select a collection within PebbleGo (animals, science, biographies, social studies, or health). Within the collection, we select a category, then a subcategory, and then an article. Each time we make a selection together, I draw attention to the breadcrumb that is created at the top of the databases. Students quickly learned how to navigate the database using the breadcrumbs at the top.

The strategy's basic steps are:

1. Introduce students to the central themes in a story.
2. Demonstrate an informational search.
3. Connect the fictional story with the search.
4. Point out the navigational features that allow users to visualize and retrace their path.

I decided to use this strategy when I noticed that many of my students were not using the breadcrumbs to navigate within PebbleGo. Instead of simply going back one breadcrumb, they would click the Home button and then have to navigate through the collection to the subcategory once again. After learning to use the navigational strategy, students are using PebbleGo more independently—and efficiently.

This case can be expanded to align with the strategies in the Four Corners Framework, as Table 7.6 demonstrates.

TABLE 7.6 Case Study 6: Alignment with the Four Corners Framework

INTEGRATION	The librarian saw a gap when he noticed that students were not navigating independently within the database.
CULTURE	Once students learn to use breadcrumbs for navigation in the library, they can use the same skills in their classrooms with their teacher or at home.
MODELING	The librarian used verbal modeling to explain how the breadcrumbs let the class retrace their path.
MENTORSHIP	Students can participate in peer mentorship by explaining to each other how they got to a page in the database so that others can also find it.

CASE STUDY 7
Lateral Reading

We (Katie and Connie) have been implementing integrated digital literacy instruction on lateral reading or reading across tabs to locate, evaluate, verify, and compare information sources. This strategy encourages students to corroborate the credibility, intent, and biases of an author or source by searching for credentials of the sources and articles on the same topic by other writers. Lateral reading teaches students how to locate, evaluate, and interpret information by requiring them to leave the original website to explore whether a claim can be verified in multiple resources. Lateral reading often requires the students to have multiple tabs open at once as they verify sources.

> **PROGRAM INFORMATION**
>
> **GRADE LEVEL:**
> 9th–12th grade
>
> **SUBJECT AREA:**
> Library
>
> **LESSON AUTHORS:**
> Katie Fisher and Connie King
>
> **LOCATION:**
> Liberty, Missouri
>
> **ISTE DIGITAL SKILLS:**
> Locate information, evaluate sources, and interpret information
>
> **ISTE STANDARD FOR EDUCATORS:**
> Citizen 2.3.b
>
> **TECHNOLOGY TOOLS INTEGRATED:**
> Wikipedia (wikipedia.com), research databases, and other topic-related sources

We began using this strategy after noticing that students tended to rely on the first search hit when conducting research. Lateral reading requires students to find information in multiple sources and think critically about which sources are the most accurate and timely. Lateral reading requires students to look beyond that first source and explore multiple resources to verify claims. This approach empowers students to use encyclopedic sources such as Wikipedia to build background knowledge, and then to move beyond these sources to find verifiable and reliable information. As we teach lateral reading, we have noticed students organically asking questions about their sources, moving beyond sources such as Wikipedia, and evaluating sources using tools to check credibility. Overall, lateral reading is a valuable tool that enables students to develop critical thinking skills, evaluate information effectively, and become more discerning consumers of information.

Lateral reading can be used for both internet-based research and database research. The ability to find resources that verify each other and reflect common themes helps students locate effective keywords, understand their research at a deep level, evaluate their own understanding of a topic, and synthesize information from various sources.

During the early phases of student research, we teach them how to use lateral reading for evaluation of sources by telling them to:

- Scroll beyond the first links. Use sites like Wikipedia for background information. Go deeper to find citable sources.
- Ask yourself: Is the website credible? Who produced or wrote the information? Is the information biased? To check, open a tab or click live links to search the author. Read laterally about the author and source.
- Ask yourself: Are the sources within the site trustworthy? To check, click links embedded in the text to open in new tabs, and read laterally across the tabs to look at the references used in your source.
- Compare sources: Find multiple sources about the same topic. Does the information in any one source differ from the information in the other sources? Triangulate your information, or find similar research information in at least three different sources and evaluate for credibility through lateral reading.

Scan the QR code to see the graphic organizer we use to support lateral reading instruction.

This case can be expanded to align with the strategies in the Four Corners Framework, as Table 7.7 demonstrates.

LATERAL READING ORGANIZER

TABLE 7.7 *Case Study 7: Alignment with the Four Corners Framework*

INTEGRATION	The librarians saw a gap when they noticed that students were relying on the first search they found.
CULTURE	Once students learn to do lateral reading in the library, they can use it when working in other classes.
MODELING	The librarians used verbal modeling to show how to do lateral reading using multiple tabs and exploring multiple resources.
MENTORSHIP	Librarians mentor teachers to support students using lateral reading in their classes.

CASE STUDY 8
Accessing Research in a Filtered School

How many times has an article or resource you needed for teaching been blocked by internet filters? Designed to protect students from accessing obscene images and content that could be harmful to minors (Anderson, 2016), these content filters are required by law (CIPA). Most high schools use content filters on in-school or school-issued devices, like laptops and iPads, but many schools overfilter, often blocking legitimate instructional content that students may be asked to read, watch, or view by teachers.

PROGRAM INFORMATION

GRADE LEVEL:
9th–12th grade

SUBJECT AREA:
All

LESSON AUTHOR:
Jenna Kammer

LOCATION:
Warrensburg, Missouri

ISTE DIGITAL SKILLS:
Evaluate sources, navigate technology ecosystems

ISTE STANDARD FOR EDUCATORS:
Facilitator 2.6.b

TECHNOLOGY TOOLS INTEGRATED:
Internet filters, school library databases, such as EBSCOhost

Students tend to use workarounds to reach the content, such as accessing the site from their phones, bypassing the filters via a VPN, or even hacking their computers. Not all students have access to working, connected, or charged mobile devices at all times, however, nor do they always make the extra effort to access blocked content needed for class.

Learning how to bypass an internet filter is a natural curiosity for students! This simple strategy encourages that in wholesome and healthy ways by introducing the library database as a workaround. While articles or videos on the web may be blocked by school internet filters, the school library database is not subject to those filters and will retrieve reliable sources on the same search topic from its curated contents. For example, articles on the biological process of reproduction in plants or animals may be blocked by school internet filters due to key words they find. This can be difficult for biology students who need to cite articles for a project or read them as required class readings. The library database, however, will likely have many articles within their resource collections on the same topics which are available in full text.

The simple strategy of modeling how to access research on library databases, even to find an article that's blocked in an internet search, teaches students to use the library databases to access information. You can model this for students by showing them the search on the internet and also in the databases. Here are few tips that teachers can use to make this work:

- Talk to school librarians to find out what digital resources are available in the library related to your subject.
- Ask the librarian to model how to use the library resources so that you can model their use to students.
- Take a few minutes to show students how to find a needed resource in the library databases. Allow them to see how you access the databases, what search terms you use, and how they can save the article.

Using this simple strategy, students learn about internet filters and understand why some content might be blocked. This conversation may lead to discussion of security, algorithms, and content filtering online. In addition, students learn to use library databases, which are important digital resources that are often under utilized. The information available in databases is often of better quality and may not be freely available on the web. Understanding that these library resources exist—not only in their high school but also college and public libraries—and are useful can prepare students for doing research as part of lifelong learning.

This case can be expanded to align with the strategies in the Four Corners Framework, as Table 7.8 demonstrates.

TABLE 7.8 Case Study 8: Alignment with the Four Corners Framework

INTEGRATION	The teacher works with the school librarian to learn what resources are available to integrate them into the class.
CULTURE	The librarian understands what digital resources are needed and can secure their access, as well as support students who seek help for using them in the library.
MODELING	The teacher models to students how to use the library databases to find relevant articles, including search terms to use and strategies for saving relevant sources.
MENTORSHIP	The librarian has served as a mentor to the teacher by supporting the use of the library databases for access and research.

CASE STUDY 9
Five-Minute Tips to Teach Digital Literacy

Jana Gerard, coordinator of the EDvolution Center in the College of Education, Health and Human Studies at Southeast Missouri State University, prepares new teachers to integrate technology in the classroom through the frameworks of the ISTE Standards for Educators and the 4Cs of Future Ready Learning. The simple digital literacy strategies that follow are some of the many she teaches her students to use in their future classrooms. Crossing content areas and spanning grade levels, the strategies all take less than five minutes to share with students and can be easily incorporated into existing lessons.

PROGRAM INFORMATION

GRADE LEVEL:
K–12th grade

SUBJECT AREA:
All

LESSON AUTHOR:
Jana Gerard

LOCATION:
Southeast Missouri State University, Cape Cirardeau, Missouri

ISTE DIGITAL SKILLS:
Locate information, evaluate sources, interpret information, express ideas, communicate with others, navigate technology ecosystems

ISTE STANDARD FOR EDUCATORS:
Citizen 2.3.b

TECHNOLOGY TOOLS INTEGRATED:
Various

Strategies for All Ages

Remind students that their passwords are like their toothbrush: They don't want to share!

Have students "THINK" before they share online by asking themselves if what they're about to share or post is:

- **T**ruthful
- **H**elpful
- **I**nspiring
- **N**ecessary
- **K**ind

Make sure students "mind their manners" even online. Digital etiquette, also known as *netiquette*, is important, and students sometimes need reminders about basic skills for being polite during digital communication, such as:

- Typing in all caps is interpreted as shouting.
- Those reading their digital messages can't see their facial expressions or hear their tone of voice. Sarcasm is easily misinterpreted.
- Humor is contextual and does not always come across as intended in digital communication.
- Digital communication is based on audience and purpose. Have students think about how formal or informal their digital communication needs to be, and ask themselves: Who am I communicating with? What is my relationship with them?
- What information am I communicating?

Strategies for Elementary Students

Any time students will be navigating the web to search for information, remind them to double-check before they click. Tell them "Check before you click!" and suggest they ask themselves:

- Is this an ad?
- Does this have anything to do with what I'm searching for?
- Is this a way to trick me into clicking on something I don't need to click on?

To help students evaluate sources and content, have them ask themselves:

- Can I trust this information?
- Can I easily read the information, or are there a lot of words that I must skip while I read this?
- Are there charts or images to help me understand this information?
- Where does this information come from? Is it a .gov or .edu site versus a .com site?
- Who is the author or creator? Do I know who this is?
- Is this information supported by other websites or books?
- Does the information on the website fit what I already know about the topic?

Strategies for Secondary Students

Ask students: Are your passwords secure? Then share basic password best practices with students, such as don't use the same password for every account and longer passwords are better. Explain how passphrases can help them remember multiple passwords and longer passwords. Passphrases are basically sentences that build on things easy to remember, like a favorite movie or book, that allows for uppercase, lowercase, numbers, and symbols, such as B@tm@nlives!nGoth@mCity23.

To help students provide appropriate attributions and credits (especially for visual content), tell them about Google's quick way to search images and videos for Creative Commons licensing:

1. Type what you need an image or video of, like *giraffes*.
2. Click Images or Videos.
3. Click Tools.
4. Click Usage Rights, then choose Creative Commons licenses.

Remind students that their actions online leave a trail that adds to their *digital shadow* (images and text on the web that they may not know exist, like untagged pictures on a school website), their *digital footprint* (their online presence, such as their social media or browsing history tracked by cookies), or their *digital tattoo* (pieces of their digital identity that cannot be erased and live permanently on the web).

Compare how students appear online to a piece of paper: "When you get a new piece of paper, it's clean and unwrinkled. After you crumple the paper, drop it on the floor, and step on it a couple of times, it's no longer clean and unwrinkled when you pick it up. Your digital presence is like that piece of paper. You can do some work to clean it up if it gets crumpled and smudged, but it's easier to keep clean from the start."

At the beginning and end of each semester, give students these helpful tips to "spring clean" their digital presence:

- Search yourself in your web browser.
- Check your privacy settings on all your social media sites and various devices (privacy settings can be different on mobile devices versus desktops).
- Make sure your passwords are secure.
- Keep your software and hardware updated on all your devices.
- Delete apps you're no longer using.
- THINK before you post!
- Use your online presence as a force for good.

This case can be expanded to align with the strategies in the Four Corners Framework, as Table 7.9 demonstrates.

TABLE 7.9 Case Study 9: Alignment with the Four Corners Framework

INTEGRATION	Teachers can integrate any of these strategies into their lessons. For example, when students are entering their password, a teacher can ask them to consider a passphrase that helps them to remember it.
CULTURE	Teachers can share the tips that work with other teachers. For example, teachers can share with specialists how they are teaching the class to "mind their manners" to encourage the same behaviors in other settings.
MODELING	Teachers can model any of these strategies to students when they are teaching. For example, a teacher could use enthusiastic modeling of the THINK strategy before sharing something online.
MENTORSHIP	Teachers can seek mentorship from other technology experts in the building for new ideas.

Chapter 7 Takeaways

In this section, the important takeaways from the chapter are paired with the ISTE Standards for Educators that inform them.

- Teachers can use common classroom phrases and mneumonics to integrate digital literacy throughout the day and within other content areas. This can help to build a culture of digital literacy in and out of the classroom (Citizen 2.3.b).
- Connecting students with digital resources, while modeling how to use them, helps students to think more critically about information, while also improving their instructional practice (Designer 2.5.b).
- Providing students with opportunities to create media allows them to learn to use resources, troubleshoot technology (solving their own problems), and deepen learning in an active way (Facilitator 2.6.d).

Reflection

Before moving on, take some time to consider how the ideas in Chapter 7 apply within your context using the questions below.

- Which case study resonated most with you and your goals for your classroom?
- What gaps did the case studies help you recognize or give you ideas to address?
- Explore some of the strategies shared. Was there a specific strategy that resonated with you? Why?

CHAPTER 8
Designing Digital Literacy Experiences

KEY ISTE STANDARDS

This chapter addresses the ISTE Standard for Educators:

- Designer 2.5.a, 2.5.b, 2.5.c

By the end of this chapter, you will:

- Consider how you might design your own digital literacy experiences within your content area.
- Use the Four Corners Framework to increase digital literacy instruction.

Designing Digital Literacy Instruction

Throughout this book, we have shared many examples for teaching digital literacy within subject areas. These examples show how teachers and librarians can improve students' digital literacy skills—locating information, evaluating sources, interpreting information, expressing ideas, communicating with others, and navigating technology ecosystems—while using simple instructional strategies.

In this chapter, we will share a lesson plan template to help you identify your own opportunities for increasing digital literacy for your students. We don't intend that you will need to redevelop any lessons plans or even take time away from core concepts you already teach. Instead, we suggest looking for opportunities that already exist to incorporate simple strategies for teaching digital literacy. Think of this lesson plan template as more of a practice in considering what opportunities already exist for developing skills that may be deficient.

The following steps use the ADDIE model of instructional design, which is useful for developing educational training programs. The ADDIE model is a widely accepted five-step approach (Dick & Carey, 2004; Morrison, 2010) that helps the instructor think about the instruction from stages of:

- Analysis
- Design
- Development
- Implementation
- Evaluation

We have adapted this model for teachers as a general framework to help you think through the design process of including digital literacy in existing instruction. Though these steps are linear, they do not need to be inflexible.

Stage 1: Identify Gaps

The first step to designing for digital literacy is to identify the areas in which your students need more skills. Where do you notice that students would benefit most from improved digital literacy? For example, would they do better on research projects if they had more instruction on using library databases? Would the sources they choose for the projects be of increased quality if they learned to use lateral reading to evaluate information? Would they be more likely to use ebooks if they understood the navigational features they could use to support their learning?

For documentation purposes, you can determine where your identified gap aligns with digital literacy skills and what mental habits are needed to develop these skills.

Example: An English teacher notices that students are using random webpages, many without even authors or dates, as resources for their papers. Students could benefit from developing evaluation skills, using the mental habit of thinking critically to evaluate sources as they find them.

Stage 2: Identify Learning Opportunities

Once the gap is identified, consider what learning objectives you might implement related to digital literacy specifically. This is not meant to be a learning objective for the overall lesson but is instead meant to improve the results of the overall lesson. For example, what measurable learning objectives might help students to do better on their papers? Writing a digital literacy goal as a measurable learning objective can help teachers to know later if that goal was met.

Example: The English teacher writes a measurable objective that students will be able to find at least two peer-reviewed sources to cite the content in their paper.

Stage 3: Determine the Teaching Strategy

Once the goal is set, consider which teaching strategies might work best to move students toward this goal. Could integrating learning experiences help to improve digital literacy? Or modeling? Mentoring? Could you pull from the digital culture in the school to improve this learning goal? In this stage, you may need to develop new resources or make plans to implement the strategy.

Example: Using the Four Corners Framework, the teacher thinks about the different ways that they can help students to reach this learning objective.

Stage 4: Implement the Strategy

In the fourth phase, you can implement the plan you developed in Stage 3. This may involve integrating several strategies or all of them, or even just one at a time. In this stage the actual delivery of the teaching strategies occurs. During this stage, note what is happening with students' digital literacy as the different strategies occur.

Example: The English teacher uses digital culture and invites the school librarian to give a presentation on the different resources related to the paper that are available in the library. The librarian also models how students may find them, and then students mentor each other as they search for resources. Observations are noted.

Stage 5: Evaluate the Strategy

The last part of the design process is to do an informal evaluation of how digital literacy was improved through the strategies applied. Because this should not be an additional step than what is already happening within the flow of the classroom, you can look at what is already being produced by students to see if there are improvements. For example, are they showing greater understanding when talking about information resources? If there are improvements, then digital literacy has increased! If not, then go back to the drawing board as a reflective practitioner and consider if there are other strategies which may be applied in other areas.

Example: The English teacher is grading the research papers students submitted and can find two peer reviewed sources in each paper. The digital literacy intervention was successful!

Designing Digital Literacy Guide

Use the following template as a guide to help outline your ideas.

Stage 1: Digital Literacy Skill to Develop (Choose as many as apply)	• Locating information • Evaluating sources • Interpreting information • Expressing ideas • Communicating with others • Navigating technology ecosystems • Mental habit needed:
Stage 2: Measurable Objective	Students will…

Stage 3: Teaching Strategy (Pick 1–4; describe)	Integrate	Culture	Model	Mentor

Stage 4: Implement Strategy	Observation notes:
Stage 5: Analyze	Did students meet the digital literacy goals? Yes No

References

Abraham, A. (2022). Why copying code is the masterclass of learning how to code. *Medium.* medium.com/codex/why-copying-code-is-the-masterclass-of-learning-how-to-code-85083c7a136d

Abraham Lincoln gives life lessons [Digital image]. (2021). knowyourmeme.com/memes/people/abraham-lincoln/photos

Agarwal, P. K., Roediger, H. L., McDaniel, M. A., & McDermot, K. B. (2020). How to use retrieval practice to improve learning. Washington University in St. Louis. pdf.retrievalpractice.org/RetrievalPracticeGuide.pdf

Anderson, E. M., & Shannon, A. L. (1988). Toward a conceptualization of mentoring. *Journal of Teacher education, 39*(1), 38–42.

Anderson, M. (2016, April 22). How internet filtering hurts kids. *The Atlantic.* www.theatlantic.com/education/archive/2016/04/internet-filtering-hurts-kids/479907

Aqili, S., & Moghaddam, A. (2008). Bridging the digital divide: The role of librarians and information professionals in the third millennium. *Electronic Library 26*(2), 226–237.

Audrin, C., & Audrin, B. (2022). Key factors in digital literacy in learning and education: A systematic literature review using text mining. *Education and Information Technologies,* 1–25.

Bakhshaei, M., Hardy, A., Ravitz, J., & Seylar, J., (2020, April). Instructional coaching holds promise as a method to improve instruction with technology. *Society for Information Technology & Teacher Education International Conference,* 1616–1625. Association for the Advancement of Computing in Education (AACE).

Bandura, A. (1997). *Self-efficacy: The exercise of control.* Freeman & Company.

Bandura, R. & Méndez Leal, E. (2022). The digital literacy imperative [report]. Center for Strategic & International Studies. www.csis.org/analysis/digital-literacy-imperative

Bennett, S., Maton, K., & Kervin, L. (2008). The 'digital natives' debate: A critical review of the evidence. *British journal of educational technology, 39*(5), 775–786.

Bergdahl, N., Fors, U., Hernwall, P., & Knutsson, O. (2018). The use of learning technologies and student engagement in learning activities. *Nordic Journal of Digital Literacy, 13*(2), 113–130.

Boser, U. (2013). Are schools getting a big enough bang for their education technology buck?. *Center for American Progress.* www.americanprogress.org/article/are-schools-getting-a-big-enough-bang-for-their-education-technology-buck

Brod, G. (2021). Predicting as a learning strategy. *Psychonomic Bulletin & Review, 28*(6), 1839–1847.

Bruff, D. (2022, December 20). *Three things to know about AI tools and teaching.* Agile Learning. derekbruff.org/?p=3970

Carillo, E. (2019). *The MLA guide to digital literacy*. The Modern Language Association of America.

Carter, S., & Andersen, C. (n.d.). *Well-being in educational contexts*. usq.pressbooks.pub/wellbeingineducationalcontexts/chapter/chapter-1

Caulfield, M. (2017). *Web literacy for student fact-checkers*. Pressbooks. pressbooks.pub/webliteracy

Cazaly, L. (2021, September 10). How to save yourself from "information overload." *Harvard Business Review*. hbr.org/2021/09/how-to-save-yourself-from-information-overload

Coding with Elias (2021). *How to make a Google homepage using HTML and CSS* [Video]. YouTube. youtu.be/ZY1MYwUDZsY

Cooke, N. (2018). *Fake news and alternative facts*. ALA Editions.

Cooper, B. (2016, April 22). It's time for the digital tattoo. *Simple K12*. www.simplek12.com/digital-citizenship/its-time-for-the-digital-tattoo

Costa, A. L. (n.d.). *Habits of mind*. www.habitsofmindinstitute.org/hear-art

Davis, V. (2014). *Reinventing writing*. Routledge.

Denbo, S. (2016). On being a historian today: The importance of digital literacy. *Perspectives on History*. www.historians.org/research-and-publications/perspectives-on-history/summer-2016/on-being-a-historian-today-the-importance-of-digital-literacy

Dick, W., & Carey, L. (2004). *The systematic design of instruction*. Allyn & Bacon.

Ertmer, P. A., & Ottenbreit-Leftwich, A. (2013). Removing obstacles to the pedagogical changes required by Jonassen's vision of authentic technology-enabled learning. *Computers & Education*, 64, 175–182.

Eshet, Y. (2004). Digital literacy: A conceptual framework for survival skills in the digital era. *Journal of educational multimedia and hypermedia*, 13(1), 93–106.

Figueroa, M. A. (2018). Futuring for future ready librarians. *Knowledge Quest*, 46(4), 14–18.

Fingal, J. (2022). Digital citizenship: From don'ts to do's to seamless integration. ISTE. www.iste.org/explore/digital-citizenship/digital-citizenship-donts-dos-seamless-integration

Fisher, D., & Frey, N. (2008). *Better learning through structured teaching: A framework for the gradual release of responsibility*. Association for Supervision and Curriculum Development.

Florida Center of Instructional Design. (2019). Technology integration matrix (3rd ed.). fcit.usf.edu/matrix/matrix

Frazier, K. (2022). Should educators introduce VR to their digital literacy lesson plans? www.kaixr.com/post/digital-literacy-lesson-plans

Frey, B. B., Lohmeier, J. H., Lee, S. W., & Tollefson, N. (2006). Measuring collaboration among grant partners. *American Journal of Evaluation*, 27(3), 383–392.

Friesem, Y. (2015). *On becoming a digital literacy mentor: Self-determination and media production in elementary education*. University of Rhode Island.

Gentry, L. B., Denton, C. A., & Kurz, T. (2008). Technologically-based mentoring provided to teachers: A synthesis of the literature. *Journal of Technology and Teacher Education*, 16(3), 339–373.

REFERENCES

Giles, M., Baker, S. F., & Willis, J. M. (2020). Pre-service teachers' peer mentoring experience and its influence on technology proficiency. *Mentoring & Tutoring: Partnership in Learning, 28*(5), 602–624.

Gilster, P. (1997). *Digital literacy*. Wiley.

Gökdas, F., & Çam, A. (2022). Examination of digital literacy levels of science teachers in the distance education process. *Educational Policy Analysis and Strategic Research, 17*(2), 208–224.

Gonzalez, J. (2017). Teaching students to legally use images online. *Cult of Pedagogy*. www.cultofpedagogy.com/online-images

Hague, C., & Payton, S. (2011). Digital literacy across the curriculum. *Curriculum Leadership, 9*(10).

Hattie, J. (2009). *Visible learning for teachers*. Routledge.

Hattie, J. (2023). *Visible learning: The sequel*. Routledge.

Hays, L., & Kammer, J. (2021a). *Integrating digital literacy in the disciplines*. Stylus Publishing.

Hays, L., & Kammer, J. (2021b). Teaching computer science: An exploration of habits of mind. *The Advocate, 27*(1), 4.

Hays, L., & Kammer, J. (2023). A new resource on digital citizenship. *C2C Digital Magazine, 1*(18), Article 1. scholarspace.jccc.edu/c2c_online/vol1/iss18/1

Hendy, H., & Raudenbush, B. (2000). Effectiveness of teacher modeling to encourage food acceptance in preschool children. *Appetite, 34*, 61–76.

Hiefield, M. & Carter, N. (2021, September 26). There is more to digital equity than devices and bandwidth. ISTE. www.iste.org/explore/education-leadership/there-more-digital-equity-devices-and-bandwidth

Hobbs, R., & Coiro, J. (2016). Everyone learns from everyone: Collaborative and interdisciplinary professional development in digital literacy. *Journal of Adolescent & Adult Literacy, 59*(6), 623–629.

Institute for Habits of Mind. (2022). *What habits of mind are*. www.habitsofmindinstitute.org

ISTE. (n.d.). *Digital skills for a global society*. www.getdigitalskills.org

ISTE. (2017). ISTE Standards: Educators. www.iste.org/standards/iste-standards-for-teachers

ISTE. (2023). ISTE Standards: Coaches. www.iste.org/standards/iste-standards-for-coaches

ISTE. (2023). *Session 1*. ISTE certification course. Online.

James, J. (2011). Technology, coaching, and community. *Learning & Leading with Technology, 39*(2), 48.

Kaminsky, M. (2023, May 11). How to copyright a photograph or image. *LegalZoom*. www.legalzoom.com/articles/how-to-copyright-a-photograph-or-image

Kammer, J., Schuler, K., & Hays, L. (2023). What do preservice teachers know about teaching with technology? International Society for Technology in Education (ISTE), Annual Conference, Philadelphia.

Kennedy, G. E., Judd, T. S., Churchward, A., Gray, K., & Krause, K. L. (2008). First year students' experiences with technology: Are they really digital natives?. *Australasian Journal of Educational Technology, 24*(1), 108–122.

Kim How, R., Zulnaidi, H., & Rahim, S. (2022). The importance of digital literacy in quadratic equations, strategies used, and issues faced by educators. *Contemporary Educational Technology, 14*(3), 1–17.

King, M., & Kammer, J. (2023). School library-led community engagement. *Knowledge Quest*, March/April.

Kirschenbaum, M. (2017a, January). *How savvy are your students: 7 fake websites to really test their evaluation skills*. EasyBib. www.easybib.com/guides/7-fake-websites-to-test-students

Kirschenbaum, M. (2017b, February). *Identifying fake news: An infographic and educator resources*. EasyBib. www.easybib.com/guides/evaluating-fake-news-resources

Kirschner, P. A., & De Bruyckere, P. (2017). The myths of the digital native and the multitasker. *Teaching and Teacher Education, 67*, 135–142.

Klein, A. (2021). During COVID-19, schools have made a mad dash to 1-to-1 computing. What happens next? *Education Week*. www.edweek.org/technology/during-covid-19-schools-have-made-a-mad-dash-to-1-to-1-computing-what-happens-next/2021/04

Knight, J. (2007). *Instructional coaching: A partnership approach to improving instruction*. SAGE Publications.

Lai, C. (2015). Modeling teachers' influence on learners' self-directed use of technology for language learning outside the classroom. *Computers & Education, 82*, 74–83.

Lang, J. (2021). *Small teaching*. Jossey-Bass.

Lang, R., Shogren, K. A., Machalicek, W., Rispoli, M., O'Reilly, M., Baker, S., & Regester, A. (2009). Video self-modeling to teach classroom rules to two students with Asperger's. *Research in Autism Spectrum Disorders, 3*(2), 483–488.

List, A. (2019). Defining digital literacy development: An examination of pre-service teachers' beliefs. *Computers & Education, 138*, 146–158.

Manfra, M., & Holmes, C. (2020). Integrating media literacy in social studies teacher education. *Contemporary Issues in Technology and Teacher Education, 20*(1), 121–141.

Mattson, K. (2017). *Digital citizenship in action*. ISTE.

McClintock Miller, S., & Bass, B. (2019). *Leading from the library: Help your school community thrive in the digital age*. ISTE.

McDougall, J., Readman, M., & Wilkinson, P. (2018). The uses of (digital) literacy. *Learning, Media and Technology, 43*(3), 263–279.

McGrew, S., Breakstone, J., Ortega, T., Smith, M., and Wineburg, S. (2018). Can students evaluate online sources? Learning from assessments of civic online reasoning. *Theory & Research in Social Education. 46*, 165–193.

Megowan-Romanowicz, C. (2016). What is modeling instruction? *NSTA Reports, 3*.

Mentoring Resource Center. (2008). *Building effective peer mentoring programs in schools: An introductory guide*. educationnorthwest.org/sites/default/files/building-effective-peer-mentoring-programs-intro-guide.pdf

Methe, S. A., & Hintze, J. M. (2003). Evaluating teacher modeling as a strategy to increase student reading behavior. *School Psychology Review, 32*(4), 617–622.

Miller, M. (2022). *Mind, motivation and meaningful learning strategies for teaching adult learners*. ALA editions.

Mishra, P., & Koehler, M. (2006). Technological pedagogical content knowledge: A framework for teacher knowledge. *Teachers College Record, 6*, 1017–1054.

Missouri Department of Elementary and Secondary Education. (2016). K–5 ELA Missouri Learning Standards: Grade-level expectations. dese.mo.gov/media/pdf/curr-mls-standards-ela-k-5-sboe-2016

Moorefield-Lang, H., & Craddock, I. (2023, March). Technology connections. Teaching students about their digital legacies. School Library Connection. schoollibraryconnection.com/content/article/2296537

Moorefield-Lang, H., & Lang, J. (2020). Keeping your digital legacy safe. *Library Technology Reports*, *56*(5), 29–31.

Morrison, G. R. (2010) *Designing effective instruction*. John Wiley & Sons.

Mullen, C. A., & Klimaitis, C. C. (2021). Defining mentoring: A literature review of issues, types, and applications. *Annals of the New York Academy of Sciences*, *1483*(1), 19–35.

Munteen, P., & Wallace, G. (2023). This program is using VR training to help solve the nationwide mechanic shortage. CNN. amp-cnn-com.cdn.ampproject.org/c/s/amp.cnn.com/cnn/2023/02/16/tech/mechanic-training-vr/index.html

Nearpod Team. (2023). How to strengthen your I do, we do, you do lessons with technology. Nearpod Blog. nearpod.com/blog/how-to-strengthen-your-i-do-we-do-you-do-lessons-with-technology

Newsela, Inc. (n.d.) *Newsela*. newsela.com

Ng, W. (2011). Why digital literacy is important for science teaching and learning. *Teaching Science*, *57*(4), 26–32.

Nunes, L. D., & Karpicke, J. D. (2015). Retrieval-based learning: Research at the interface between cognitive science and education. *Emerging trends in the social and behavioral sciences*, 1–16.

OECD & Eynon, R. (2020). The myth of the digital native: Why it persists and the harm it inflicts. In Burns, T. and F. Gottschalk (eds.), *Education in the Digital Age: Healthy and Happy Children*. OECD Publishing. doi.org/10.1787/2dac420b-en

Ottenbreit-Leftwich, A., & Kimmons, R. (2018). *The K–12 educational technology handbook* (1st ed.). EdTech Books.

Palmer, P. (2007). *The courage to teach* (10th anniversary ed.). John Wiley & Sons.

Pangrazio, L., Godhe, A. L., & Ledesma, A. G. L. (2020). What is digital literacy? A comparative review of publications across three language contexts. *E-learning and Digital Media*, *17*(6), 442–459.

Patson, N. D. (2021). Collaborative note-taking as an alternative to recording online sessions. *Faculty Focus*. www.facultyfocus.com/articles/online-education/online-assessment-grading-and-feedback/collaborative-note-taking-as-an-alternative-to-recording-online-sessions/?utm_campaign=shareaholic&utm_medium=copy_link&utm_source=bookmark

PBS Learning Media (2015). The future of digital learning. d43fweuh3sg51.cloudfront.net/media/media_files/PBS-LearningMedia-The-Future-of-Digital-Learning-Infographic.jpg

Peng, D., & Yu, Z. (2022). A literature review of digital literacy over two decades. *Education Research International*, *2022* (Article 2533413). doi.org/10.1155/2022/2533413

Picton, I., Clark, C., Riad, L., & Cole, A. (2022). Insights into young people's literacy, critical digital literacy, online communication and wellbeing. National Literacy Trust. cdn.literacytrust.org.uk/media/documents/Literacy_critical_digital_online_communication_wellbeing_2021_mYxoTGi.pdf

Pilgrim, J., & Vasinda, S. (2021). Fake news and the "wild wide web:" A study of elementary students' reliability reasoning. *Societies, 11*(4). doi.org/10.3390/soc11040121

Plymouth State University. (2023). *General education*. coursecatalog.plymouth.edu/general-education

Polizzi, G. (2020). Digital literacy and the national curriculum for England: Learning from how the experts engage with and evaluate online content. *Computers & Education, 152*, 103859.

Predicting. (n.d.). Let's talk science. letstalkscience.ca/educational-resources/learning-strategies/predicting

Prensky, M. (2001). Digital natives, digital immigrants. *On the Horizon, 9*(5), 1–6.

Puentedura, R. (2006). *Transformation, technology and education: A model for technology and transformation*. hippasus.com/resources/tte/puentedura_tte.pdf

Ribble, M. (2017). *Nine elements*. Digital Citizenship. www.digitalcitizenship.net/nine-elements.html

Rideout, V. J., & Katz, V. S. (2016). Opportunity for all? Technology and learning in lower-income families. A report of the Families and Media Project. New York: The Joan Ganz Cooney Center at Sesame Workshop. digitalequityforlearning.org/wp-content/uploads/2015/12/jgcc_opportunityforall.pdf

Roose, K. (January, 2023). Don't ban ChatGPT in schools. Teach with it. *The New York Times*. www.nytimes.com/2023/01/12/technology/chatgpt-schools-teachers.html

Ryu, J., Kim, Y. A., Eum, S., Park, S., Chun, S., & Yang, S. (2022). The assessment of memes as digital multimodal composition in L2 classrooms. *Journal of Second Language Writing, 57*, 100914.

Samuel, A. (2017). How librarians can be digital mentors for teens. *JStor Daily*. daily.jstor.org/how-librarians-can-be-digital-mentors-for-teens

Sánchez-Cruzado, C., Santiago Campión, R., & Sánchez-Compaña, M. T. (2021). Teacher digital literacy: The indisputable challenge after COVID-19. *Sustainability, 13*(4), 1858.

Sirlin, N., Epstein, Z., Arechar, A. A., & Rand, D. G. (2021). Digital literacy is associated with more discerning accuracy judgments but not sharing intentions. *Harvard Kennedy School Misinformation Review 2*(6), 1–13.

Smith, A. (2018). 4 ways to teach students to find the gems in YouTube's perilous terrain. In *Edtech for the K–12 Classroom*. ISTE.

STEM Learning Design. (2022). Massachusetts Digital Literacy and Computer Science Curriculum. www.doe.mass.edu/stem/dlcs/curriculum-guide.pdf

Stenger, M. (2018). 7 ways to teach digital literacy. InformEd. www.opencolleges.edu.au/informed/edtech-integration/7-ways-teach-digital-literacy

Suber, P. (2012). *Open Access*. MIT Press Essential Knowledge Series. direct.mit.edu/books/oa-monograph/3754/Open-Access

Sweller, J. (2020). Cognitive load theory and educational technology. *Educational Technology Research and Development*, 68(1), 1–16.

Thomas, S., Howard, N. R., & Schaffer, R. (2018). *Closing the gap: Digital equity strategies for the K–12 classroom*. ISTE.

Tinmaz, H., Fanea-Ivanovici, M., & Baber, H. (2022a). A snapshot of digital literacy. *Library HiTech News*, (ahead-of-print).

Tinmaz, H., Lee, Y-T., Fanea-Ivanovici, M., & Baber, H. (2022b). A systematic review on digital literacy. *Smart Learning Environments*, 9(21). **doi.org/10.1186/s40561-022-00204-y**

Thompson, C. (2014). *Smarter than you think: How technology is changing our minds for the better*. Penguin.

Top, E., Baser, D., Akkus, R., Akayoglu, S., & Gurer, M. D. (2021, January). Secondary school teachers' preferences in the process of individual technology mentoring. *Computers & Education*, 160, 104030.

United States Department of Education. (2015). Characteristics of future ready leadership: A research synthesis. Office of Educational Technology. **tech.ed.gov/files/2015/12/Characteristics-of-Future-Ready-Leadership.pdf**

United States Department of Education (2021). CARES Act Emergency Relief. **www.ed.gov/coronavirus/cares-act-emergency-relief**

van Dijk, J., & Hacker, K. (2003). The digital divide as a complex and dynamic phenomenon. *Information Society*, 19(4), 315–326.

Wang, J. (2001). Contexts of mentoring and opportunities for learning to teach: A comparative study of mentoring practice. *Teaching and Teacher Education*, 17(1), 51–73.

Wells, M., Hestenes, D., & Swackhamer, G. (1995). A modeling method for high school physics instruction. *American Journal of Physics*, 63(7), 606–619.

Yu, J., Karakaya, O., & Schmidt-Crawford, D. A. (2018). Mentoring for success: Graduate student mentors' perceptions on the impact of a one-on-one technology mentoring program. *Proceedings of Annual Convention of the Association for Educational Communications and Technology*, 229–237.

Zapato, L. (1998, March 8). *Help save the endangered pacific northwest tree octopus*. Zpi. **zapatopi.net/treeoctopus**

Zilka, G. C. (2021). Attitudes, emotions, and the use of emoji in social networking apps by children, adolescents, and young adults. *Interchange*, 52(3), 337–355.

Zimmer, W. K., & Matthews, S. D. (2022). A virtual coaching model of professional development to increase teachers' digital learning competencies. *Teaching and Teacher Education*, 109, 103544.

Index

NUMBERS

3Cs in filmmaking, 96
3Ss in filmmaking, 96
4 Moves and a Habit, 34
4Cs of Future Ready Learning, 128
5th grade, analyzing news and media sources, 109–112
6th–8th grade, 120
7th & 8th grade, case study, 117–120
9 Key Ps of digital citizenship, 86–88
9th–12th grade
    Accessing Research in a Filtered School, 126–128
    AI or Human (Expert), 115–116
    Flattening the Latin Word, 113–115
    Lateral Reading case study, 124

A

Abraham, A., 83
Accessing Research in a Filtered School, 126–128. *See also* databases
accuracy, striving for, 9, 48
ADDIE model of instructional design, 134–135
administrator, collaboration with, 60
administrator-led modeling, 85
Adobe Express, 38, 117–119
Agarwal et al., 21
AI (artificial intelligence), 52
AI or Human (Expert) case study, 115–116
All4Ed schools, Digital Learning Day, 61
Anderson, M., 126
Anderson and Shannon, 104
applying knowledge to new situations, habit of mind, 48
applying past knowledge to new situations, habit of mind, 9
Aqili & Moghaddam, 57
articles and videos, generating summaries of, 35
assignment design, 42
Audrin & Audrin, 3, 5
awe and wonderment, responding with, 9, 48

B

Bakhshaei et al., 104
Bandura, A., 81, 88
Bandura & Méndez Leal, 25
Bass, William, 76
bell work, 47
Bennet et al., 6–7, 11
Bergdahl et al., 21
Blogger, 47
Boser, U., 57
Boyett, Nina, 63–64
Breakout EDU, 99
Brod, G., 21

C

Canva, using for videos, 98
Carillo, E., 43
case studies. *See also* digital literacy
    Accessing Research in a Filtered School, 126–128
    AI or Human (Expert), 115–116
    Analyzing News and Media Stories, 109–112
    The Digital Tattoo Strategy, 120–121
    Five-Minute Tips to Teach Digital Literacy, 128–131
    Flattening the Latin Word, 113–115
    Four Corners Framework, 108
    Lateral Reading, 124–126
    Making the Case for Photo Credits, 117–120
    Navigating Databases with Digital Breadcrumbs, 122–123
Caulfield, Mike, 34
Cazaly, L., 35
ChatGPT tool, 2, 35, 83, 115–116
Citizen Educator Standard 2.3 b, ISTE, 3
clarity and precision, thinking and communicating with, 48
ClassDojo, 56, 99
classroom teacher, collaboration with, 59
Closing the Gap: Digital Equity Strategies for the K-12 Classroom, 57
coding, expert modeling, 82–83
Coding with Elias, 83
cognitive load theory, 22
collaboration
    administrator, 60
    classroom teacher, 59
    and communication, 58
    between educators, 62–67
    IT (information technology) staff, 60
    school librarian, 59
    support staff, 60–61
    technology coach, 59–60
collaboration software, 36
collaborative leadership, 26
co-mentoring/collaborative mentoring, 92–93
communicating and thinking, 48
communication, 8, 36, 51, 58, 102. *See also* thinking & communicating with clarity and precision; WOVEN (Written, Oral, Visual, Electronic, Nonverbal) communication

community, building with digital experiences, 49–50
community engagement, 24
Computers and Education Open journal, 35
Connected Learning Lab, 70
connections to prior knowledge, 22
continuous learning, remaining open to, 9, 48. *See also* learning opportunities; lifelong learning
Cook, Andrea, 120
Cooke, N., 10
Cooper, David, 100, 120
cooperation, level of collaboration, 62–63
coordination, level of collaboration, 62–63
copyright, photos and images, 119
Costa, A., 8
COVID-19 pandemic, 56, 67
CRAAP (Currency, Relevance, Authority, Accuracy, Purpose) Test, 53
creating, habit of mind, 9, 48
critical digital literacy, 3–4. *See also* digital literacy
critical skills, 4
Cult of Pedagogy, 118
cultural mentoring, 92, 94
culture, Four Corners Framework, 12–13, 46, 64, 80, 94, 112, 115–116, 120–121, 123, 126, 128, 131

D

DALL·E 2 tool, 47
data, gathering through senses, 9, 48
databases, navigating with digital breadcrumbs, 122–123. *See also* Accessing Research in a Filtered School
Davis, Vicki, 86
Denbo, S., 2
Dick & Carey, 134
Dickinson, Emily, 116
digital citizenship, 9 Key Ps, 86
digital competence, identifying levels of, 39–40
digital content, creation of, 58
digital culture, strategies for building, 69–70
digital divide, 11, 57
digital equity, modeling, 88
digital etiquette, modeling, 86
digital experiences, emerging technology for, 52
digital footprint, 37, 64, 120, 130
digital inclusion, modeling, 87
digital learning culture, support for, 68–69
Digital Learning Day, 61
digital legacy, 37
digital literacy. *See also* case studies; critical digital literacy; functional digital literacy; modeling
  across disciplines, 65–66
  challenged to teaching, 56–58
  core elements, 7–11
  criticism of terminology, 56
  defined, 2–6
  design guide, 137
  versus digital citizenship, 5
  within disciplines, 64–65
  distributing in schools, 67
  emphasizing in use, 37–39
  identifying gaps, 134–135
  instructional design, 134–136
  instructional strategies, 134–136
  integration of, 50–51
  within learning system, 23–25
  mentoring programs, 103
  and misinformation, 10
  model, 4
  problem in schools, 11–12
  research about, 5–6
  skills and habits of mind, 7–8, 48
  starting with self, 32–37
  strategies, 28–30
  teaching in schools, 12–14
  teaching strategies, 20–22
  tips for teaching, 128–131

The Digital Literacy Foundation, 103
digital literate student, portrait of, 15–16
digital native, 5–6
Digital Natives, Digital Immigrants, 7
digital ownership, modeling, 87
digital security, modeling, 87. *See also* security
digital shadow, 130
digital tattoo, 37, 64
Digital Tattoo Strategy, 120–122
#digitalinclusion, 34
#digitallearners, 34
#digitalliteracy, 33
digitally literate person, defined, 7
digitally literate student, portrait of, 14–15. *See also* students
digitally literate teacher, portrait of, 14–15. *See also* educators; teachers
Dijk & Hacker, 57
Discovering Media Literacy: Digital Media and Popular Culture in Elementary School, 100
discussion groups, mentoring through, 100–101
diverse mentoring, 92–93
#DLDay, 61

E

EdSurge Podcast, 34
Edtech for the K–12 Classroom, 22
Educational Technology and Society journal, 35
educators. *See also* digitally literate teacher; ISTE Standards for Educators; teachers
  collaboration between, 62–67
  mentoring between, 95–96
ELA unit, 28
electronic mentoring, 92–93
elementary students, strategies for, 129–130
Ellipsis Education Computer Science Courses, 25
emerging technology, 52
empathy and understanding, listening with, 48
engagement, 21

English Language Arts, 109–112, 115–116
Epic database, 87
Epic! digital library, 28
Ertmer & Ottenbreit-Leftwich, 104
Eshet, Y., 6
etiquette, modeling, 86
evaluation skills, 10–11
expert modeling, 82–83

F

Figueroa, M. A., 27
filmmaking, 3Cs and 3Ss, 96
filtered school, accessing research in, 126–128
finding humor, habit of mind, 9
Fingal, J., 32
Fisher, Katie, 124
Fisher & Frey, 77
Flip tool, 99
Florida Center for Instructional Technology, 45
formal mentoring, 92–93
Four Corners Framework
  Accessing Research in a Filtered School, 128
  AI or Human (Expert), 116
  alignment with teacher-led modeling, 80
  digital literacy case studies, 108
  Digital Tattoo Strategy, 121
  Flattening the Latin Word, 115
  Hexameter.co alignment, 46
  lateral reading, 126
  and levels of collaboration, 64
  and Media Analyzer, 112
  and mentoring, 94
  Navigating Databases with Digital Breadcrumbs, 123
  parts of, 12–14
  photo credits case study, 120
  teaching digital literacy, 131
Frazier, K., 82
Frey et al., levels of collaboration, 62–63
Friesem, Y., 100
FRS (Future Ready Schools) Framework, 26–27
full collaboration, level of collaboration, 62–63
functional digital literacy, 3. *See also* digital literacy
functional skills, 4
Future Ready Schools, Digital Learning Day, 61

G

gaming, using in self-modeling, 82
gathering data through all senses, habit of mind, 9, 48
Gentry et al., 104
Georgia Tech, 65–66
Gerard, Jana, 128–131
getdigitalskills.org, 8, 33, 50
Giles et al., 96
Gilster, P., 2–3, 6, 56
Gonzalez, Jennifer, 118
Google Scholar, 34
Google Search, 118
Gorman, Amanda, 116
gradual release, 77
group mentoring, 92–93
guest speaker, 42

H

habits of mind, 8–9, 47–48
  alignment of activities, 49
  K–12 students, 10–11
  modeling, 84–85
Hague and Payton, 67
Hattie, John, 21
Hays & Kammer, 3, 36, 65, 83, 115–116
Hendy and Raudenbush, 88
Hexameter website, 45–46
Hiefield and Carter, 57
Hobbs, Renee, 100
Hobbs and Coiro, 65, 70
humor, finding, 9

I

I Do, We Do, You Do method, 77–78. *See also* modeling
ideas, expressing, 8, 36, 51, 102
IJDLDC (*The International Journal of Digital Literacy and Digital Competence*) journal, 35
images
  getting copyrights for, 119
  using legally online, 118
imagining, habit of mind, 9, 48
impulsivity, managing, 9, 48
informal mentoring, 92–93
information. *See also* misinformation
  evaluation of, 53
  interpreting, 35, 102
  locating, 101
  locating and interpreting, 8, 33–34
information literacy, 6, 58
infrastructure, 25–26
innovating, habit of mind, 9, 48
inpulsivity, managing, 9
Institute for Habits of Mind, 8–9
instructional design, 134–135
integration, Four Corners Framework, 12–13, 46, 64, 80, 94, 112, 115–116, 120–121, 123, 126, 128, 131
internet filters, 126–128
Iowa State University, 99
ISTE (International Society for Technology in Education), digital-literacy skills, 8, 32
ISTE Standards for Educators. *See also* educators
  Citizen 2.3.a, 54, 74
  Citizen 2.3.b, 3, 29, 109–115, 122, 124, 128–132
  Citizen 2.3.c, 104, 115–120
  Citizen 2.3.d, 89, 120
  Collaborator 2.4, 36, 62
  Collaborator 2.4.a, 30, 71
  Collaborator 2.4.b, 29–30
  Collaborator 2.4.d, 89
  Designer 2.5.a, 17, 46, 54, 64
  Designer 2.5.b, 132
  Designer 2.5.c, 17, 30
  Facilitator 2.6.a, 104
  Facilitator 2.6.b, 30, 126–128

ISTE Standards for Educators (*continued*)
   Facilitator 2.6.d, 29, 89, 104, 132
   Leader 2.2, 69
   Leader 2.2.a, 71
   Leader 2.2.b, 85, 96
   Leader 2.2.c, 71, 89, 104
   Learner 2.1, 32, 39, 100
   Learner 2.1.a, 54
   Learner 2.1.b, 104
   Learner 2.1.c, 17, 30, 54
ISTELive edtech conference, 34
IT (information technology) staff, collaboration with, 60

J

James, J., 104
Johnson, Ben, 45–46, 113–115
journaling, 47
Judd, Tucker, 80

K

K–5 ELA (English Language Arts), MLS, 25
K–5th grade, Navigating Databases with Digital Breadcrumbs, 122
K–12th grade
   habits of mind, 10–11
   teaching digital literacy, 128–131
Kahoot! 20–22, 56
Kai XR virtual reality teaching platform, 82
Kaminsky, M., 119
Kammer, J., 115–116, 126–128
Kammer et al., 79
Kennedy et al., 6–7
Kerr Sims, Shantia, 79–80
Keyboarding without Tears program, 25
Kim How et al., 65
King, Connie, 124
King, Matt, 122
King and Kammer, 66
Kirschenbaum, M., 111
Kirshner & De Bruyckere, 7
Klein, A., 67–68
Knight, J., 104

knowledge, applying, 9, 22, 48
knowledge system, creating, 35

L

Lai, C., 89
Lang et al., 82
Language Arts, 30
language arts & reading, 65
lateral reading, 34, 53, 124–126. *See also* reading & language arts
Latin, teaching, 45–46, 113–115
The Latina Tech Mentor program, 103
learning opportunities, identifying, 135. *See also* continuous learning
learning system, digital literacy within, 23–25
Learning Unleashed podcast, 34
librarians. *See also* public librarians
   FRL (Future Ready Librarians) Framework Crosswalk, 27
   partnering with, 42
lifelong learning, 11. *See also* continuous learning
Lincoln, Abraham, 43
List, A., 5–6
listening with understanding and empathy, 48
Lofi Girl, 75

M

Makey Makey, 99
Mallon, Megan, 109–112
managing impulsivity, habit of mind, 9, 48
Manfra & Holmes, 65
Maryland's Vehicles for Change, 78
Massachusetts Digital Literacy and Computer Science Curriculum, 25
math, 65
Mattson, K., 2
McClintock Miller, Shannon, 76
McDougall et al., 24
Media Analyzer, 111
media and news sources, analyzing, 109–112

Media Education Lab, 70
media literacy, 6
Megowan-Romanowicz, C., 84
memes, using as strategy, 43
mental habits, 4, 8
mentoring
   defined, 92
   and digital literacy skills, 101–102
   between educators, 95–96
   Four Corners Framework, 115, 120, 123, 131
   incorporating strategy of, 102–103
   programs, 103
   strategy, 92–94
   students, 97–98
   for teachers, 104
   technology, 104
   through discussion groups, 100–101
   types, 92–94
Mentoring Resource Center, 97
mentorship, Four Corners Framework, 12, 14, 46, 64, 80, 94, 112, 116, 121, 126, 128
metacognition. *See* thinking about thinking
metaverse, 52
Methe and Hintze, 88
Miller, M., 22
Mishra & Koehler, 12
misinformation, 10. *See also* information
Misinformation Solutions Forum, 53
Missouri, Show Me state, 81
Missouri Department of Elementary and Secondary Education, 142
MLS (Missouri Learning Standards), K–5 ELA, 25
modeling. *See also* I Do, We Do, You Do method
   administrator-led, 85
   digital equity, 88
   digital etiquette, 86
   digital inclusion, 87
   digital ownership, 87
   digital security, 87

Digital Tattoo Strategy, 121
Four Corners Framework, 12–14, 46, 64, 80, 94, 112, 115–116, 123, 126, 128, 131
   habits of mind, 84–85
   incorporating strategy of, 86–88
   overview, 74–75
   photo credits case study, 120
   student-led, 76, 81–85
   success case studies, 88–89
   teacher-led, 75–81
   with technology, 89
   theory behind, 88
Moorefield-Lang and Craddock, 37
Moorefield-Lang and Lang, 37
Morrison, G. R., 134
Mullen and Klimaitis, 92–93
multilevel mentoring, 92, 94
Munteen and Wallace, 78

N

Nearpod, 77, 79
netiquette, 129
networking, level of collaboration, 62–63
Newport High School, 63–64
news and media sources, analyzing, 109–112
Newsela, 109–112
Ng, W., 22
Nunes & Karpicke, 21

O

OCED & Eynon, 7
Open Access, 35
opportunities, 42, 45–49
Ottenbreit-Leftwich & Kimmon, 12

P

Pacific Northwest Tree Octopus, 111
Padlet, 51, 85
Palmer, P., 97
Pangrazio et al., 5–6
passwords, 9 Key Ps of digital citizenship, 86
Patson, N. D., 36
PBS Learning Media, 68

PebbleGo, 122
peer mentoring, 92–93
peer modeling, 81–82
Peng & Yu, 3, 5
Pengrazio et al., 5–6
permission, 9 Key Ps of digital citizenship, 86
persisting, habit of mind, 9, 48
personal, 9 Key Ps of digital citizenship, 86
personal information, 9 Key Ps of digital citizenship, 86
personal relevance, 22
personalized professional learning, 26
personalized student learning, 26
PhET simulations, 77
photo credits, making case for, 117–120
photograph, 9 Key Ps of digital citizenship, 86
photos, getting copyrights for, 119
PIC-RAT, 12
Picton et al., 65
Pilgrim and Vasinda, 109
PLCs (professional learning communities), 85, 101
PLNs (professional learning networks), 85, 101
Plymouth State University, 8–9
podcasts, 34
Polizzi, G., 3
predicting, 21
Prensky, M., 5, 7
private information, 9 Key Ps of digital citizenship, 86
problem resolution, 58
problem solving, 10–11
problems, questioning and posing, 9, 48
professional journals, 34–35
professional learning, 26
professionalism, 9 Key Ps of digital citizenship, 86
property, 9 Key Ps of digital citizenship, 86
ProQuest database, 87
protecting, 9 Key Ps of digital citizenship, 86

public librarians, 103.
   See also librarians
Puentedura, R., 12, 44–45

Q

QR codes
   Connected Learning Lab, 70
   Georgia Tech's WOVEN approach, 66
   Lateral Reading Organizer, 125
   lateral vs. vertical reading, 53
   Media Education Lab, 70
   Misinformation Solutions Forum, 53
   SIFT tutorial, 53
questioning and posing problems, habit of mind, 9, 48

R

Raudenbush, B., 88
reading & language arts, 65.
   See also lateral reading
relationship skills, developing, 82
remaining open to continuous learning, habit of mind, 9
reporting perspectives, evaluating, 35
responding with wonderment and awe, habit of mind, 9, 48
retrieval strategies, 20–22
Rexhausen, Tiffany, 117–120
Ribble, M., 109
Rideout and Katz, 66
risks, taking responsibly, 9, 48
Rita Allen Foundation, 53
Roose, K., 83
Ryu et al., 43

S

SAMR (Substitution, Augmentation, Modification, Redefinition), 12, 44–45
Samuel, A., 103
Sánchez-Cruzado et al., 58
school librarian
   collaboration with, 59
   role of, 27
school strategies, 24
Schoology, 37

science, 65
secondary students, strategies for, 130–131
security, 58. *See also* digital security
self-awareness skills, developing, 82
self-modeling, 82
Show Me state, Missouri, 81
SIFT Method, 34
SIFT tutorial, 53
silent peer modeling, 82
Sirlin et al., 10
situational understanding, 11
Slido, 77
Smarter Than You Think, 35
Smith, Adrienne, 22
social studies, 65
socio-cultural perspectives, 6
software, evaluating, 39
sources, evaluating, 8, 34–35, 101, 126–128
STEM (science, technology, engineering, math), 84
STEM Learning Design, 25
Stenger, 25
strategies. *See also* memes
  building digital culture, 69–70
  evaluating, 136
  examples, 28–30
  implementing, 135–136
  memes as, 43
striving for accuracy, habit of mind, 9, 48
Strutin, Ryan, 98
student learning. *See* personalized student learning
student-created models, 84
student-led modeling, 76, 81–85
students. *See also* digitally literate student
  asking to use and teach digital literacy, 41
  determining digital literacy skills of, 49–50
  experiences, 24
  influences on, 23
  mentoring students, 97–98
  mentoring teachers, 98–100
  showcasing digital literacy skills, 42
Suber, Peter, 35
support staff, collaboration with, 60–61
Sweller, J., 22

T

taking responsible risks, habit of mind, 9, 48
teacher-led modeling, 75
teachers. *See also* digitally literate teacher; educators
  mentoring students, 96–97
  students mentoring, 98–100
teaching
  practices, 25
  strategies, 20–22, 135
"Teaching Students to Legally Use Images Online," 118
tech support needs, reducing, 68–69
technology
  emergence of, 52
  mentors, 104
  and self-modeling, 82
technology coach, collaboration with, 59–60
technology ecosystems, navigating, 8, 37, 51, 102, 120, 122, 126–128
technology use, considerations, 66–67
THINK strategy, 129
thinking & communicating with clarity and precision, habit of mind, 9, 48. *See also* communication
thinking about thinking, habit of mind, 9, 48
thinking flexibly, habit of mind, 9, 48
thinking interdependently, habit of mind, 9, 48
Thomas, et al., 57
Thompson, C., 35
Tinmaz et al., 6
Top et al., 95
"Toward a Conceptualization of Mentoring," 104
TPACK, 12

U

understanding and empathy, listening with, 48
University of California, Irvine, 70
University of Central Missouri, 79

V

van Dijk & Hacker, 57
vertical reading, 53
videos, using Canva for, 98
videos and articles, generating summaries of, 35
visibility, 21
VR (virtual reality), 52, 77–78

W

Wang, J., 92
Wells et al., 84
Wikipedia, 124
Wiktionary, 113–115
wonderment and awe, responding with, 9, 48
words composed daily, number of, 35
WOVEN (Written, Oral, Visual, Electronic, Nonverbal) communication, 65–66. *See also* communication

Y

The Youngster.co program, 103
Yu et al., 99

Z

Zapato, L., 111
Zilka, G. C., 99
Zimmer & Matthews, 94